black dog
publishing
london uk

EVERYDAY SPECIALS
CAFES & TEAROOMS

GRAND AFFAIRS
AFTERNOON TEA

POP IN, TAKE OUT
BAKERIES & PASTISSERIES

TEA WITH A TWIST
ALTERNATIVE & THEMED

VIRTUOUS VICES
VEGAN & ALLERGY-FRIENDLY

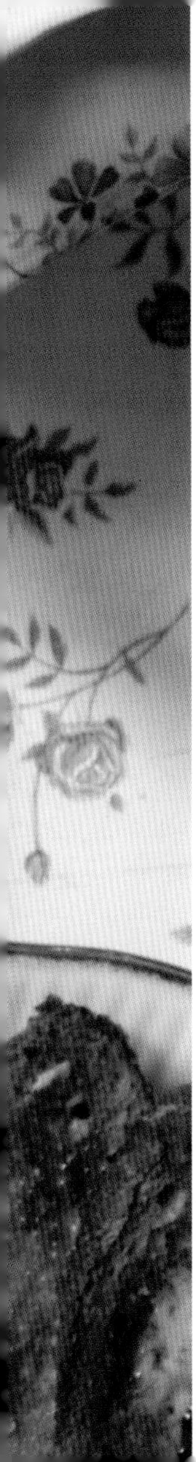

INTRODUCTION

It was after a particularly awful tea and cake experience that I began looking for a book about the best places to stop for tea in London. Although magazines, websites and general foodie books had covered some ground, it was impossible to find a guide solely dedicated to teatime destinations in the capital. I became fixated on rooting out these prized places myself and, before long, the pastime grew from a casual search for quality tea and cake, to a public and shared celebration of establishments that offered a direct challenge to our greying world of chains.

As I began working on this guide, I noticed the city's interest in tea and cake was blossoming, and new independents were cropping up and flourishing all over town. One lucky encounter led to another and I began to develop a catalogue of cafes and tearooms manned by owners, bakers and pastry chefs who care about the quality of food they serve and the environment in which they serve it. From this ever-burgeoning list the very best places have been cherry-picked for *Tea & Cake London* and the book offers a broad taste of what the capital has to offer, from frills-free, contemporary cafes to ultra-fancy hotels bolstered by decades of history. Across five chapters, I have introduced my personal favourites and little-known gems, as well as acknowledged iconic London institutions that enjoy international regard. Throughout the guide, you will find thriving local tearooms, upmarket spots for afternoon tea, quick-stop bakeries, oddball recommendations and a growing number of cafes dedicated to specialist diets. In all cases, I have hoped to avoid the dull, the staid and the uninspired and suggest something for special days when you just cannot face those over-familiar high street options.

The choice here also recognises and celebrates our growing pride in British culture and the revival of long-overlooked traditions. Taking tea is an age-old ritual, and the glorious delight of digging a fork into a soft, buttery sponge and pouring a hot brew from the pot has hardly dampened over the decades. Teatime continues to refresh and entertain and it is comforting to know that, in such a frenetic city and during such fast-paced times, everything can still stop for tea.

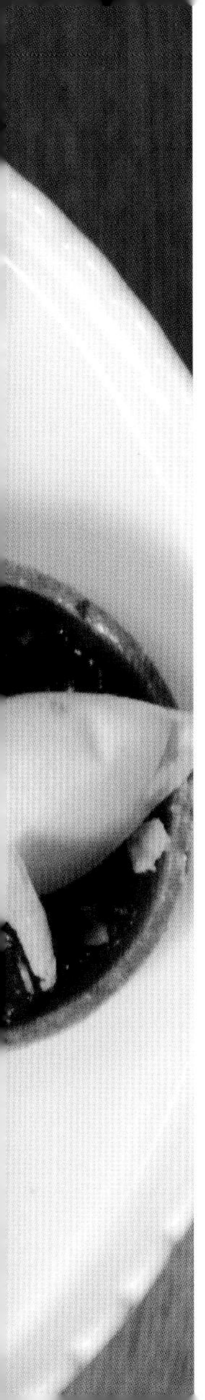

EVERYDAY SPECIALS

CAFES & TEAROOMS

At the turn of the twentieth century—at a time when wealthy Londoners were enjoying refined afternoon teas in upmarket hotels—the working classes were becoming partial to high street tearooms. J Lyons & Co was famed for this service, opening its first London tearoom in 1894 and expanding its chain to more than 200 branches. Staffed by nippies (waitresses in black and white aproned uniforms), the smart bakery-cafe establishments catered for all, and their popularity helped Britons cement their love of taking tea. Since then, our thirst for tea has had its peaks and troughs, surviving the changing fashions of cafe culture and reemerging with force recently as we look to give a nostalgic nod to the past. "Everyday Specials" celebrates long-loved London tearooms as well as new cafes looking to recapture the magic of traditional British teatime. This chapter also notes exemplary forward-thinking cafes together with teahouses that focus on the pleasure of fine loose leaves and the ceremony of serving an exceptional brew. Regardless of style, these entries are about recognising the plentiful stops across London that offer the chance to refresh your spirit with an impromptu teatime.

London Review
Cake Shop
Rose and
Pistachio
Gluten Free

LONDON REVIEW CAKE SHOP

14 Bury Place, WC1A 2JL
www.lrbshop.co.uk
020 7269 9045

Ideally located, but not ideally sized, this diminutive central London cafe has more fans than it is able to deal with. Being part of the London Review Bookshop, its tables are usually filled with quiet readers, academics, writers and the odd stray tourist who has found their way over from the nearby British Museum. Yet despite its popularity, the cafe remains a serene spot, and if you find yourself a seat, it warrants the squish.

The menu shares much of the same independent, well-informed spirit of the Bookshop itself, with cakes including a lemon, rosemary and olive oil sponge that oozes citrus juices; and a less-soggy pistachio and rose. If these bakes sound like they have arrived via North Africa, it is because owner Terry Glover and her team are heavily influenced by the region's fragrant, spiced and rustic style of baking. Glover is also a fan of intriguing teas, and orders a strong selection from notable supplier Jing. There are a couple of vanilla combinations on the menu that go especially well with a sweet slice; or for a black tea with a difference, go for the smoky Keemun Mao Feng with its chocolaty notes. If you order a white, green or oolong tea, you will be served a boxed, bamboo tray with a glass teapot and cup—a nod to China's traditional gongfu style of service. It is a lovely quirk that adds a distinctly meditative quality to the teatime proceedings.

J+A CAFÉ

4 Sutton Lane, EC1M 5PU
www.jandacafe.com
020 7490 2992

With such an elusive address, it is hard to fathom quite how J+A Café has become so popular. That is, until you try it. Set just off the rough-and-tumble of Clerkenwell Road (though best accessed via Great Sutton Street), the cafe occupies a former diamond-cutting factory on a historic London lane—finding it feels like you have unearthed a wonderful city secret. Indoors, the striking industrial building—all exposed brick walls, large windows and high ceilings—has been lovingly turned into a cafe by sisters Johanna and Aoife Ledwidge and their hands-on family. Their Irish background can be felt in the menu, which stars superlative Irish soda bread (best eaten with lashings of jam) and hearty soups and stews.

Try to avoid the lunchtime rush and root out this treasure at teatime, when whole cakes, loafs, scones and brownies are out to tempt. The cooking style comes largely from Darina Allen and the method of her Ballymaloe Cookery School based on an organic farm in Ireland. So expect comfort cakes for cold days such as a syrupy apple and maple sponge or a velvety chocolate and Guinness number. Dig in with a pot of tea courtesy of Mighty Leaf Tea or the well-established J Atkinson & Co, which has been trading since 1837.

PURE CEYLON TEA
t-sips
LOVERS LEAP
Single Estate
Garden Fresh Tea

PURE CEYLON TEA
t-sips
LOVERS LEAP

Single Estate
Garden Fresh Tea

PURE CEYLON TEA
t-sips
ADDAWATTE
Single Estate
Garden Fresh Tea

PURE CEYLON TEA
t-sips
LOVERS LEAP

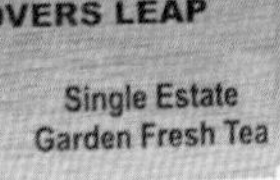
Single Estate
Garden Fresh Tea

PURE CEYLON TEA
t-sips
LOVERS LEAP

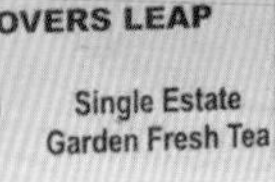
Single Estate
Garden Fresh Tea

LANKA

71 Regent's Park Road, NW1 8UY
www.lanka-uk.com
020 7483 2544

Under the skilled hand of head chef Masayuki Hara, Lanka is where the best of French, British and Japanese patisserie meet. Hara cut his teeth at some of London's finest restaurants before opening this petite Primrose Hill cafe to serve impeccably executed confections and a short but carefully chosen lunch menu.

The thrill of Lanka is its originality. All the familiar French sweets are here, and a few British ones too, but they have been rendered exceptional by sheer culinary creativity. A bread and butter pudding, for example, is made with brioche instead of bread, giving it a luxe character. Elsewhere, Japanese ingredients are used with aplomb. There is jasmine in the crème brûlée; green tea powder in the hypnotically good chocolate cake as well as azuki bean in the white chocolate gateau. Macaroons may look a little on the dull side, but their muted shades are down to a welcome lack of artificial colouring.

Teas are just as important as the cakes here, and Lanka works with Sri Lankan tea salon Euphorium to provide quality blends and infusions. The Royal Delight, a black tea with floral and fruity notes, is the ideal accompaniment to sweet food. For something with a kick, opt for Vitality—a heady, herbal mix of citrus, liquorice and chicory root.

PEGGY PORSCHEN

116 Ebury Street, SW1W 9QQ
www.peggyporschen.com
020 7730 1316

With a cult following, Peggy Porschen is undoubtedly the doyenne of sugarcraft. The German pastry chef has worked in some of the top kitchens in the UK and her complex and creative cakes have earned her superstar fans such as Elton John and Stella McCartney. Wedding cakes are her forte, and her princess-pink cake parlour in Belgravia houses a bridal boudoir where brides-to-be can book an appointment to chat flavours, icing and personalised design. For the rest of us, there is the parlour itself, a girlie boutique where poodle-shaped biscuits with white icing sit alongside darling cupcakes in pastel colours.

It may be feminine, but there is nothing sickly-sweet about the cakes. Unusual ingredient combinations make the cupcakes stand out—flavours include limoncello; white chocolate and passion fruit; banoffee (with a banana jam centre); and orange truffle. With a nod to her roots, Porschen also does a dazzling Black Forest cupcake with cherry liquor kirsch in the cream cheese frosting.

Her teas hint at an obsession with sweet stuff too, and Blends for Friends (aka tea expert Alex Probyn) has helped create infusions inspired by the chef's kitchen. So you get a smooth and mellow Caramel tea as well as Orange Flower (an Earl Grey with more vibrant than normal citrus notes), Gingerbread (a sweet and spicy Masala chai) and Floral Rose.

MARBLE CAKE
SCRUMPTIOUS CARROT
BLACK FOREST
STICKY TOFFEE

POSTCARD TEAS

9 Dering Street, W1S 1AG
www.postcardteas.com
020 7629 3654

Part store, part teahouse, Postcard Teas is one of London's most prized specialists. Single estate teas and blends from more than 30 different international producers are sold here, each individually selected by founder Tim d'Offay who travels the world in search of small-scale, independent estates and makers who use traditional, artisan techniques. His emphasis on quality and sustainability works to highlight the importance of where teas come from, as well as the age of the trees and how their leaves are picked and processed. Once back in London, d'Offay continues to treat the beverage with a respect difficult to find elsewhere in the capital.

For customers looking to try before they buy, taster brews are made with exacting water temperatures and specific infusion times. Even if you are uninterested in purchasing a full caddy, you are welcome to settle at a long wooden bar and sample from a diverse menu. No food is served, but staff will generously provide a plate if you have brought your own cake. Or for tea on the go, head over to Borough Market where d'Offay has joined forces with fellow aficionado Alex Fraser to sell loose leaves under brand name, East Teas.

HIGH TEA OF HIGHGATE

50 Highgate High Street, N6 5HX
www.highteaofhighgate.com
020 8348 3162

There are few places in London more picturesque than Highgate Village. Georgian and Victorian buildings line the bustling high street and hilltop views look out over Hampstead Heath. Suitably nestled among a row of independent shops, High Tea of Highgate only embellishes the quaint picture with its pale pink front, stripy awning and homemade bunting.

Georgina Worthington gave up a career in fashion to open this well-loved cafe and serves classics such as a bouncy Victoria sandwich and mild lavender cake. These wonderfully traditional bakes, together with old-fashioned service-with-a-smile and a delightfully whimsical interior, make this one of the most traditional and pretty places to enjoy a slice of cake in London. Georgina has good taste in teas too, creating several blends especially for the cafe. Why not forsake your usual cup of English Breakfast in favour of a pot of the fragrant and gently sweet Almond Tea, or the floral and lady-like Miss Worthington's Rose Tea blended with rose petals and oil.

HIGH
TEA
of
Highgate
HIGH
TEA
of
Highgate
ROOIBOS VANILLA

PARTY

TANGERINE DREAM CAFÉ

Chelsea Physic Garden, 66 Royal Hospital Road, SW3 4HS
www.chelseaphysicgarden.co.uk
020 7349 6464

London's oldest botanic garden was always going to be an enchanting spot for a cafe, but when Limpet Barron and David Hughes converted the site's former schoolroom, no one could have foreseen their runaway success. From humble, makeshift beginnings, the Tangerine Dream Café is now a destination in its own right, tempting the green-fingered as well as non-gardeners to Chelsea Physic Garden's walled lawns and onto the cafe's lovely terrace.

Simple recipes and fresh ingredients are at the heart of the couple's menu, in which they aim to reflect the changing garden at their window. Herbs and flowers are often used in their baking (the lavender scones are a perennial feature) and seasonal fruits are relied upon to transform basic tarts. The history of the garden, which was founded by apothecaries in 1673, is also a key inspiration and finds an outlet in lemon possets, charlottes and jellies. This traditional slant is part of what makes Tangerine Dream Café (open only from April to the end of October) feel like nestling into an old friend's kitchen, leaving it a delightful place to while away an afternoon.

ROSE BAKERY

Dover Street Market, 17–18
Dover Street, W1S 4LT
020 7518 0680

The food at Rose Bakery is wholesome, natural, modest and, because of the laid-back attitude in the kitchen, never served quite the same way twice. It seems incongruous, then, to find the cafe occupying the same space as Comme des Garçons on the fourth floor of Dover Street Market, a cutting-edge concept store founded by Japanese designer Rei Kawakubo. The combination of sharing tables, earthen crockery and rails of minimalist clothing actually works well, with Rose Carrarini's pared down, unfussy culinary style reflecting Kawakubo's simple cuts, colours and designs.

Rose and her husband Jean-Charles are great champions of unpretentious cooking and when the couple founded London's Villandry back in 1988, they realised their ethos was popular with diners too. Though no longer associated with that deli-restaurant, they continue to create a homely, British menu at Rose Bakery, using responsibly sourced produce at both the flagship cafe in Paris and the London outpost.

Be warned: queues build steadily for Saturday brunch, while weekdays find shoppers and cake-lovers alike clamouring over the cafe's individually turned out carrot cakes and the simple sticky toffee pudding—Rose's personal favourite

LE CHANDELIER

161 Lordship Lane, SE22 8HX
www.lechandelier.co.uk
020 8299 3344

There is no shortage of pleasing cafes in East Dulwich, but Le Chandelier deserves special mention for the sheer diversity of tea and cake on offer. Owner Daphne Kellett enlisted Edward Eisler, the founder of tea specialist Jing, to help create a 30-strong loose leaf tea menu that provides something for every palate. The cakes, meanwhile, are a riotous collection of delicate fruit tartlets, complex chocolate gateaux, familiar British sponges and allergy-friendly options.

If choosing a tea and a slice is bewildering, cut down the decision making by going for a reasonably-priced afternoon tea. Or swap the teapot for a glass of wine or Champagne. Either way, you will be lounging under a couple of dozen chandeliers (they are available to buy, should the fancy take you) in a room that consciously brings together design elements from the tearooms of North Africa, France and Britain. It is a wonderfully stylised environment in which to indulge, though for a more casual destination in East Dulwich look out for the artisan Luca's Bakery at 145 Lordship Lane, or the cutely chic vegetarian cafe Blue Brick at 14 Fellbrigg Road.

Le Chandelier
MINT SCENTED TEA
Moroccan Mint
HERBAL INFUSIONS
Whole Rosebuds

BANANA
BUTTERMILK
SLICE 2.50
GINGER
MOLASSES
SLICE 2.50

VIOLET

47 Wilton Way, E8 3ED
www.violetcakes.com
020 7275 8360

You would be a lucky passer-by if you stumbled across Violet. Hidden away on the residential Wilton Way, this cafe-bakery relies almost entirely on its reputation for imaginative recipes and a retro atmosphere. Owner Claire Ptak, a former pastry chef for Alice Waters at the legendary Chez Panisse restaurant in Berkeley, first tickled the taste buds of East London via her stall on Broadway Market, creating something of a stir with her salt caramel cupcakes and ginger molasses cake. The Californian went on to open this Hackney shop, giving her American-influenced baking a cosy second home. Pop in and you will find Claire and her helpers sending flour flying from a large open workstation, while a vintage cabinet houses seasonal-inspired treats from rhubarb-filled scones to a coconut cream sponge.

The shop itself is tiny, but there is just enough space to sit at a window-side Formica table. Or take your hot brew, courtesy of Postcard Teas (see pages 18–19) or MayKing Tea, upstairs to the spacious seating area. If the sun is out, the mini back garden is the place to bite into one of Violet's renowned whoopie pies and sip on the house lemonade made with Amalfi lemons and soda water.

'VIOLET'
LOAF

CAKES
Coffee
espresso
Cappuccino
flat white
latte
Piccolo
Filter Coffee
French Press
Tea
breakfast
earl grey
red cloud (black)
jasmine pearls (white)
golden lily (oolong)
pu'erh (pu'erh)
rooibos (red)
buckwheat
mint or verbena
Savoury + Toast

BETTY BLYTHE

73 Blythe Road, W14 0HP
www.bettyblythe.co.uk
020 7602 1177

Black and white photos of 1920s starlet Betty Blythe hang behind the counter at this appealing kitchen and pantry. The actress may have been edgy and erotic in her time, but her namesake is more sugar than spice. Whitewashed furniture, pink bunting and vases of flowers lend the space an innocent air. As do the prams parked outside by mums sipping tea in the bright ground floor shop or joining a children's party (complete with dressing-up box) in the intimate downstairs space.

There are organic meat and eggs to buy, together with high-end larder products, but the focus here remains firmly on tea and cake. Timeless British recipes are baked and delivered daily from a local bakery, and loose leaf tea arrives from the excellent specialist Sherston Tea Company.

You would do well to sip politely with your pinky out, as Betty Blythe likes nothing better than to espouse the art of taking tea. Tips on how to throw your own tea party and a guide to etiquette and manners can be found on each table, and Betty Blythe also offers its own afternoon tea menu—very popular with hen parties.

Yumchaa
Notting Hill
Ingredients:
Apricot, Strawberry,
Marigold Blossom, Cornflowers
Black Tea. 100g
www.yumchaa.com
Yumchaa
Wanderlust
Ingredients:
Apple pieces, Almond slices,
Cinnamon and Vanilla
Green tea. 100g
www.yumchaa.com
Yumchaa
Berry Berry
Nice
Ingredients:
Rooibos, Blueberry, Blackberry,
Strawberry, Rhubarb, Kiwi,
Vanilla pieces and Rose petals
Red Tea. 100g
www.yumchaa.com

YUMCHAA

91/92 Camden Lock Place, Upper Walkway,
West Yard, NW1 8AF
www.yumchaa.co.uk
020 7209 9641

You will find a genuine passion for tea at the ever-growing Yumchaa, a brand that first found its feet when economists Trinh and Sean struggled to find a decent brew in the city. The couple decided to plug the supply gap themselves and embarked on a global search for the perfect tea during the early noughties. Today the pair continue to build on the success of their fledgling market stall in Camden, setting up further market outlets for their loose leaves as well as several branches of the Yumchaa cafe. The popularity of the latter rests largely on the ability of the founders, and the family-like Yumchaa team, to make tea exciting, accessible and as instantly gratifying as coffee.

The staff will buzz as they talk you through their personally designed blends. The exclusive, experimental creations include a gingery Gentle Giant, the vivacious Soho Spice, fiery Chilli Chilli Bang Bang, and a fruity, grassy Enchanted Forest; tea purists, meanwhile, can indulge in the Tea Master single estate range. Homemade cakes are available too (the dense, loaded fruit cake is exceptionally good) and most are made by friends and family of the founders—a crew who also help sandblast furniture, paint walls and decorate each time a new Yumchaa outlet opens.

FLEET RIVER BAKERY

71 Lincoln's Inn Fields, WC2A 3JF
www.fleetriverbakery.com
020 7691 1457

Perched on the edge of a pretty public green, Fleet River Bakery is a haven in Holborn; a slice of independent chic in something of a soulless spot. Here, cakes clamour for attention (replaced entirely by quiches, sandwiches and soups during the lunch service) on the wooded counter and Irish pastry chef Emma Farrell does a handsome job of making each one look special. She does a zingy banana and pineapple cake with mellow mascarpone icing as well as a confidently turned-out chocolate torte, carrot cake and billowing scones.

Teas come from specialist Emeyu and exciting blends could entice even a hardened coffee drinker: try resisting a Summer Bird, a refreshing fusion of lemongrass, lavender and peppermint, or Leaping Tiger, a vibrant white tea infused with mango and cornflowers.

The space itself has character too: high ceilings and three separate rooms in neutral and olive tones offer spacious calm for its mix of local professionals, LSE students and lost tourists. Large artworks fill the walls and reclaimed furniture looks smart rather than scruffy. It is an ambience nicely conceived by couple Lucy Clapp and Jon Dalton—the latter well versed in setting up effortlessly cool venues, having already masterminded Americana hot spot, Bloomsbury Bowling Lanes.

croissant
chutney & rocket
jam & rocket
Sandwich
Hummingbird Cake
Banana Walnut Cake
Jam Flapjack

FLEET RIVER BAKERY
71 LINCOLNS INN FIELDS

BREAKFAST / LUNCH / CAKES

ALL MADE FRESH
DAILY IN OUR KITCHEN

MONMOUTH COFFEE

WINE

SEATING

FLEET RIVER
HOT CHOCOLATE FESTIVAL

PRIMROSE BAKERY

69 Gloucester Avenue, NW1 8LD
www.primrosebakery.org.uk
020 7483 4222

This cutesy cafe opened its doors in 2004—the same year as The Hummingbird Bakery (see pages 138–139) and was a huge champion of the cupcake, instantly winning Londoners over with its American style. Today, it quietly goes about its baking business, serving up mini iced cakes in this original branch, as well as the more sleek-looking Covent Garden outpost. Here, the aesthetic is that of a 1950s US hang-out with Formica tables and pastel tones.

The menu is retro too, starring coke floats and peanut butter cookies. Primrose Bakery co-founders Martha Swift and Lisa Thomas like to experiment with flavours, but in the main, cupcakes are as sweet as they can be and feature traditionally American ingredients from malt and marshmallow to maple and pecan. To wash the sugar down, order a pot of Tea Pigs tea—the brand's liquorice and mint blend is divine—or carry your cake out and pop across the road to the superb deli Melrose and Morgan for a bracing, takeaway Monmouth coffee.

WELCOME!
T.A@
WITH·BUTTER £1·50
WITH·MARMITE/VEGEMITE £1·70
WITH·MARMALADE £1·70
WITH·PEACH/PLUM
WITH·PEANUT-BUTTER £1·70
JAM £1·70
WITH·HONEY £1·70
2
CRUMPETS
VANILLA
WITH SPRINKLES 1 SCOOP
2 SCOOP
FRUIT SALAD £3·40p
WITH YOGHURT £3·40p
GRANOLA WITH FRUIT AND YOGHURT £3·40p
Coke
FLOAT £3·50
GLASS OF ORGANIC
COLD MILK
£1·25
ICE
CREAM

TINA, WE SALUTE YOU

47 King Henry's Walk, N1 4HN
www.tinawesaluteyou.com
020 3119 0047

A hit among Dalston folk in the know, Tina, We Salute You is a pleasant escape from the hubbub of Kingsland Road. The cake selection is not massive, but what is available deserves attention. Soft iced vanilla cupcakes are classy rather than garish, a Victoria sandwich provides a safe choice and a white chocolate and cardamom tart leaves something for the more adventurous. There is often a hot dessert served daily during winter so you can look forward to specials such as warmed banana bread with Marsala-baked pears. The tea menu is also brief, but shines for its focus on fresh herbs (the mint tea is basically a large glass heaving with handfuls of leaves) and a fragrant flowering jasmine tea.

A square communal table fills most of the small space and its centrepiece—a tray of jams and condiments—lend the cafe a convivial vibe. Art, too, adds a living room element, and is a big part of the ethos here. Owners Steve Hawkes and Danny Hilton like to keep the place looking interesting by inviting artists to literally decorate the walls on a two month rotation. Murals, large-scale illustrations and hanging installations have all featured.

Orange and Poppy Seed
Tiger Cake
Ham and cheese
£ 3.75
Egg and herring
£ 3.50
Pickled herring
£ 3.75
Prawn

NORDIC BAKERY

37b New Cavendish Street, W1G 8JR
www.nordicbakery.com
020 7935 3590

The Nordic Bakery may well be a visual master class in functional, minimalist interiors—all tidy Scandinavian furniture, muted colours, bare walls and shades of dark wood—but beyond the stylish design there is a cafe that beats with Nordic soul. Finnish founder Jali Wahlsten set out to bring traditional pastries, cakes and sandwiches to multicultural London, favouring modest baking over elaborate recipes. So, you get simple dark rye sandwiches (a Scandinavian staple) and cakes Nordic mums might bake. Dig into a Tiger (a sort of marble cake), an orange and poppy seed sponge or the very Swedish Tosca—a soft cake topped with a crispy layer of caramel and almond.

There is no twist or fancy flourish, instead the bakery prides itself on familiar, everyday recipes. This is especially true of the cinnamon buns. The Finnish take on the bun is sweeter and packed with more flavour than the buns of neighbouring countries and, comparatively speaking, is also a touch lighter. It is still a substantial beast, however, and if you have one in place of your morning croissant, you won't hear a peep from your belly until lunch.

Tea is not a major priority here, but the Spanish blend of Dibar coffee should keep you going too. Head to this Marylebone branch for calm surrounds; if you are in town there is also a Nordic over at Soho's Golden Square.

Nordic Bakery
Coffee

YTT
TILLMANS of SWEDEN
Organic Cordial
RHUBARB
ELDERFLOWER
LINGONBERRY
Lingonsaft
dilute to taste
RASPBERRY & BLUEBERRY
LINGONBERRY
ARCTIC CLOUDBERRY

Dark rye
bread
£2.50
Dark rye
quartet
£2.50
Dark rye
organic
£3.00

THE HABERDASHERY

22 Middle Lane, N8 8PL
www.the-haberdashery.com
020 8342 8098

The Haberdashery has real community spirit. The cafe's now legendary Barboot evenings (where the space is given over to craft and vintage stalls, and teamed with a bar service) have united the area, with other shops following suit to make the idea a regular local event. The cafe also works with the out-of-town Church Farm, offering customers a chance to order produce from the grower, which is then delivered to the cafe weekly. It is touches like these that have seen The Haberdashery win a place in the heart of Crouch End residents.

The food, of course, is another winning factor. Owners Greg and Massimo (from Philadelphia and North Italy respectively) value fresh food made from locally sourced ingredients, and their French chef does a superb job of creating a lively international menu. Feathery muffins baked in Edwardian terracotta pots and a cinnamon heavy honey cake contrast kid-friendly bakes such as a peanut butter cake, wickedly loaded with nutty spread and topped with chocolate. Order a pot of W Martyn tea for a little gravitas (the tea merchant has been trading leaves since the late nineteenth century) and settle on deliberately ramshackle reclaimed furniture or the picnic benches in the leafy back garden.

If you are after a more grown-up spot, try Circus Coffee around the corner at 136 Crouch Hill. Here, deep red décor, a roaring fire, Suki teas and a slice of lemon polenta and pistachio cake should provide comfort on a rainy day.

SWISS ROLL
with
Chocolate-dipped
BRITISH STRAWBERRIES

CARROT
CAKE £3.95

EXCEPTIONAL
TEAS

TeaSmith
AFTERNOON TEA
TASTING MENU
William Curley

TEASMITH

6 Lamb Street, E1 6EA
www.teasmith.co.uk
020 7247 1333

The ceremony of tea is skillfully observed at this slick East London teahouse. There is certainly nothing cavalier about the way staff brew as you watch, using a gaiwan (a small lidded bowl) to steep a good quantity of leaves in a small amount of water. The technique means that you can get several infusions from the same leaves—perfect if you are looking to linger at the long, wooden bar. Those hoping to partake fully in this ritual should visit during the week when TeaSmith is an oasis of calm and the impressively well-informed employees have time to share their knowledge.

The weekend brings an altogether more boisterous tone to the narrow store, and you wll have to be satisfied with sharing the space with a chattering crowd. Caddies are available to takeaway and, while founder John Kennedy specialises in teas from small estates in the Far East and particularly deals in Oolong, the choice is broad.

To learn more about the range, enroll in a TeaSmith MasterClass complete with taste test and brewing experiments. Or book a more jolly Afternoon TeaSmith Ceremony where various blends are matched with biscuits, confections and cakes by master chocolatier and pâtissier William Curley. Incidentally, you can also buy TeaSmith teas (to go with extravagant chocolate cakes) at the upmarket William Curley cafe in Belgravia.

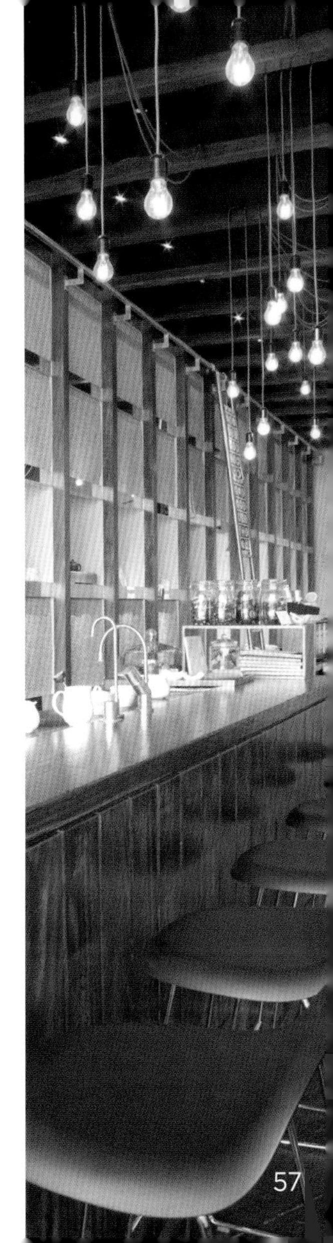

PLAIN AND FRUIT SCONES
£2 £2.30
Vanilla + chocolate orange
CUP CAKES
BOX OF 6 £10
CARROT CAKE
DAIRY FREE WITHOUT TOPPING
£2.50 £2.95
GINGERBREAD
£2.50 £2.95

THE TEA ROOMS

155 Stoke Newington Church Street, N16 0UH
www.thetearooms.org
020 7923 1870

As Londoners increasingly look to rediscover the pleasure of going out to take tea, places like The Tea Rooms are springing up in local neighbourhoods to plug the demand. The inspiration at this Stoke Newington cafe is squarely traditional British teatime and, judging by the weekend crowds, this has its appeal.

Pastry chef Isabelle Allfrey is at the helm here and her baking is plain and fuss free. That means no excessive frosting—sometimes none at all—on sponges such as lemon or ginger. A full afternoon tea is served at the weekends and the well-executed British staples feature Dundee cake and Bakewell tarts. The tea menu, sourced by High Teas, features a decent mix of blends including an interesting Green Earl Grey that uses green Chinese Gunpowder rather than a black tea base.

Half the joy at The Tea Rooms, however, is the crockery: oddly matched china pots, cups and saucers are used to serve, while items for sale are on display in dressers and along the windowsill. Allfrey's mum is in charge of sourcing these, and she is also pretty hands-on in the kitchen too, helping out with old family recipes and a touch of baking wisdom.

THE LIDO CAFE

Brockwell Lido, Dulwich Road, SE24 0PA
www.thelidocafe.co.uk
020 7737 8183

Unlike the alfresco swimming pool it looks out on, The Lido Cafe is open all year around. In public use since 1937, the Olympic-sized lido has a distinct Art Deco style and, together with its surrounding Grade II-listed building and the rolling greenery of Brockwell Park, it serves as an idyllic cafe backdrop. Make the most of the view and take tea out on the terrace during summer; or visit on a bright winter day when the blue water glistens so temptingly only the cafe's glass doors will stop you daring a dip.

Light and spacious, The Lido Cafe is a great place to idle: mothers with young children, ladies who lunch and singles wielding laptops (there is free Wi-Fi) appear to agree, and the place is often packed. The best seats in the house face the pool and the best slice to order is the flavourful, towering carrot cake. With a good citrus kick, it is one of The Lido Cafe's bestsellers and joins a wide mix of sweets from wonderful pastries and chocolate truffles from Clarke's (see pages 136–137) to excellent cookies and brownies. Enjoy with a builder's brew, bag in cup courtesy of Clipper teas.

The Lido Cafe.

FOXCROFT & GINGER

3 Berwick Street, W1F 0DR
www.foxcroftandginger.com
020 7287 5890

The banana bread at this Soho cafe may not be much to look at, but when it comes to the table lightly toasted, the banana warm and gooey, you suddenly understand why they get through 30 to 40 loaves a week. This in-house special is part of a delectable seasonal counter of sweet and savoury goodies. In autumn, expect a delicately spiced pumpkin and apple tart; in summer a lemon polenta cake. Perennial brownies are rich and nutty, and the Chelsea buns and Eccles cakes a convincing tribute to British favourites.

Teas are provided by specialist Jing—and Foxcroft & Ginger also make a memorable lemon, ginger and honey tea served with a whole lemon, a stick of ginger and oodles of honey. Drink a pot while watching the action of Berwick Street Market from the window bar, or take your cake to the basement space where battered vintage gym equipment serves as seating. Down here, the dim lighting, dark wood floors, metro tiles and mismatched antique crockery make Foxcroft & Ginger a welcome hideaway. It is a place managed with personality by a husband and wife duo Quintin and Georgina, and it confidently sets itself apart from Soho's clamouring cafe scene.

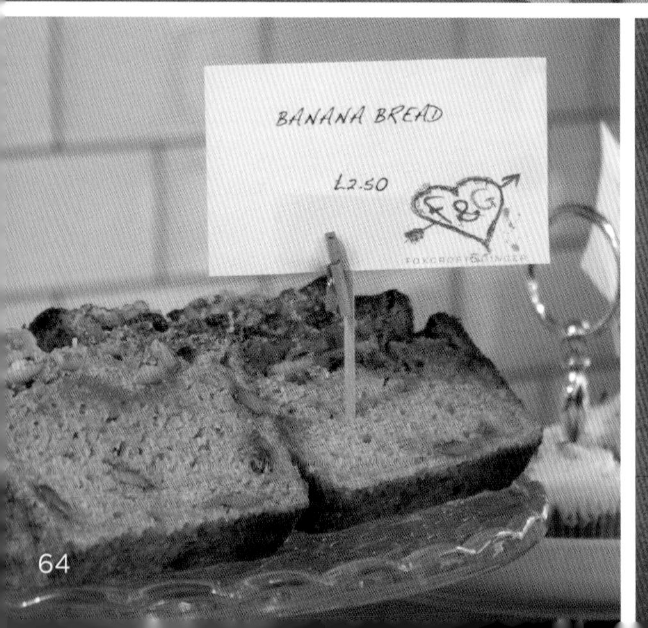
BANANA BREAD
£2.50
F&G

THE TEAHOUSE AT PETERSHAM NURSERIES

Church Lane, off Petersham Road, TW10 7AG
www.petershamnurseries.com
020 8605 3627

Located on the western fringe of Richmond Park, Petersham Nurseries is not technically in London. The area, though, is most definitely a stomping ground for weary urbanites. The Capital Ring—a popular, country-esque walking route around the perimeter of central London—skims this famed garden centre and walkers (as well as visitors to Kew Gardens and Richmond's abundant historic attractions) make a point of stopping off at its outstanding cafe or teahouse.

Acclaimed chef Skye Gyngell heads up the Michelin-starred cafe, and her soulful, seasonally-inspired food has won her a legion of fans. The Teahouse, meanwhile, has its own admirers. Much like the adjacent cafe, its home is a vast, elongated, heated greenhouse where attractively dog-eared tables are adorned with jars of cut flowers. It is a magical spot, exceptionally so come summer.

A passionate team (independent of Gyngell's kitchen) look after the menu, approaching it with care and spirit. They experiment with veggie sponges (parsnip and maple, say) and hatch upon exciting bakes—blood orange and chocolate, for instance. But they also make sure there are familiar options covering brownies, carrot cake and even the odd Victoria sandwich. Cheery staff will help you match your cake to one of their Canton Tea Co options. The award-winning brand supplies excellent Chinese teas (and a couple of Indian black blends) and also provide a "tea of the month" with which the staff look to encourage visitors to go for something new.

PETERSHAM NURSERIES

TO A TEA

14 Farringdon Street, EC4A 4AB
www.toatea.com
020 7248 3498

There is a knack to a good brew and this contemporary teahouse has boiled it down to an exact science. Knowledgeable staff will help you choose from a menu of some 30 single estate teas, fruit blends and herbal infusions, before setting a timer as your selection steeps behind the counter. This appreciated attention to detail means that, whatever you choose, you will not end up with a weak or overly bitter brew to accompany your Belgian chocolate slice or beetroot and seed cake.

Despite the quality and ample variety, tea here is pretty good value—certainly less expensive than other specialist teahouses. Perhaps this is down to the fact that To A Tea fancies itself as a Starbucks alternative, replacing the frenetic rush of cafe culture with an efficient service, affordable prices and a peaceful environment. There is something about the meticulously designed interior and modern finish that suggests, though it is independent, To A Tea is just the beginning of a chain. If so, it would be a welcome one; a worthy rival to London's many coffee outlets.

THE ART OF BREWING
TO
TEA
Rose Buds

TO
TEA

MAISON BERTAUX

28 Greek Street, W1D 5DQ
www.maisonbertaux.com
020 7437 6007

Ramshackle, bohemian and filled with personality, this local cult favourite is one of the few establishments in Soho where the past is still present. Opened in 1871 by French communards, the patisserie has seen the area change around it, moving from a seedy district via a thriving multicultural artistic hub to today's more commercial environment.

Michele and Tania Wade now run the cafe and the sisters are a suitably madcap influence. Michele is the one to consult regarding the glistening French cakes having worked at Maison Bertaux since her time as a Saturday girl back in the 1960s; Tania, meanwhile, plays art dealer and looks after the cafe's gallery. As you would expect from such an authentic eccentric, the artists she represents are a little left-field—comedian Noel Fielding, singer Jónsi Birgisson and Frank's daughter Diva Zappa have all exhibited here—and the shows are riotously hung.

The cafe's seating area is equally unruly: a wild mix of shabby furniture, personal mementos, draped pink toile and fairy lights. It makes for a fabulously lively place to stop for a Mont Blanc, a cup of tea and a bit of thespian celeb watching. Maison Bertaux is not just a cafe—it is an experience.

CAKE HOLE AT VINTAGE HEAVEN

82 Columbia Road, E2 7QB
www.vintageheaven.co.uk

Vintage Heaven is exactly what the name suggests. A paradise for rummagers, the small store is heaving with secondhand crockery, bakeware and cutlery, all lovingly sourced by its owner Margaret Willis. Meander past the precariously high piles of merchandise and through a narrow archway and you will discover Cake Hole occupying the shop's back room.

Run by Margaret's daughter Louise and her partner Mark, the quaint cafe is an ode to the 1970s. Old mirrors, paintings and framed tapestries hang on the walls, the Ercol furniture comes in various shades of brown and graphic wallpaper adds a splash of colour. Tea is served by the pot in vintage china and cakes are partially supplied by Primrose Bakery (see page 44–47), though Louise turns out a fine range of British bakes and the café's bestseller is her own coffee and walnut.

Open solely on the weekends, Cake Hole is a heaving spot on Sunday when it is busy with tourists visiting Columbia Road's famous flower market, so aim to pop by on the quieter Saturday when the cubby-like cafe really is a restful retreat.

RESERVED

Ray's Jazz Stage

CAFÉ AT FOYLES

113–119 Charing Cross Road, WC2H 0EB
www.foyles.co.uk
020 7440 3207

Loved largely for its independent spirit, Foyles was never in danger of installing a chain eaterie in its flagship bookstore. Instead, its in-house indie cafe is a perfect fit, run with care by Catherine Hadoulini, wife of Jorge Fernandez of Soho's treasured coffee house Fernandez & Wells. The cafe was once a tight squeeze, tea-drinkers sharing space with racks of jazz CDs and vinyl. But the music has since moved upstairs, making way for a host of reclaimed wooded pews and handmade tables, as well as a small stage set up for free lunchtime and evening concerts. Close ties with the London Jazz Festival, as well as an excellent programme manager, mean you are in with a good chance of seeing the next big thing (Jamie Cullum, The Puppini Sisters and Kit Downes all played here before going mainstream) though the cafe's snug atmosphere is appealing in itself.

Settle with a strong Irish brew of Barry's Tea (served caff-style in white mugs, teabag in), or a cup of Hadoulini's bespoke coffee blend made by Darlington's. Whole cakes and sweet snacks are bought in from the best artisan wholesalers and include moreish brownies and pastries (watch out for a dangerously tasty almond croissant) from Flour Power City Bakery and The Flour Station.

HURWUNDEKI

299 Railway Arches, Cambridge
Heath Road, E2 9HA
www.hurwundeki.com
020 7749 0638

Occupying a disused railway arch under Cambridge Heath station, Hurwundeki is one of the East End's more unusual cafes. Bare brick walls and the sound of trains rumbling overhead keep your location in mind, though a cup of Yumchaa tea (see pages 38–39) with one of the best custard tarts this side of Portugal will offer ample distraction. The tarts are part of a daily changing clutch of cakes, made both on site and sourced from the local, organic, eco-friendly and seasonally-inspired bakery-shop Happy Kitchen. The latter is based down the road (at Arch 402, Mentmore Terrace) and drops off healthy, veg-based cakes which are sugar and wheat-free—its carrot and coconut sponge, raspberry Bakewell tarts and double chocolate cake can be found artily-arranged on wooden boards at the counter.

The style-conscious Ki-Chul Lee (who also owns the Hurwundeki boutique and hair salon) launched with the idea of fusing an alternative shop with an alternative cafe and has brought together price-tagged bric-a-brac—think taxidermy penguins and old gramophones—with weird and wonderful furnishings, from beautiful chandeliers dripping over work-bench tables to antique tricycles out in the garden.

Yumchaa
GLUTEN FREE
Chocolate Brownies
£
ORGANIC
100% vegan!
sweetened with
No soya.
agave nectar & xylitol.

KIPFERL

20 Camden Passage, N1 8ED
www.kipferl.co.uk
020 7704 1555

After being overrun by customers at its shed-sized Barbican branch, the now relocated Kipferl has space to introduce yet more people to its exceptional Austrian cakes. The roomy Camden cafe-restaurant retains its predecessor's serene surrounds and simple, stylish design, and continues to serve an intriguing teatime menu.

The iconic Viennese Sachertorte is a must here, arriving proudly with two layers of apricot jam between the chocolate cake, giving it a substantially juicy texture. The spice-packed Linzertorte is also a great success, the almonds, redcurrant jelly, cloves and cinnamon betraying a Middle Eastern influence on the European classic. Owner Christian Malnig sticks strictly to theme here, and you will not find any British bakes among the Austrian cakes and *kipferls* (crescent-shaped almond biscuits). The distinct identity even extends to the coffee and herbal tea: the former is a mild blend from Helmut Sachers in Vienna; the latter is sourced from organic, Austrian supplier Sonnentor.

THE NATIONAL CAFÉ

East Wing, The National Gallery,
St Martin's Place, WC2N 4DN
www.thenationalcafe.com
020 7747 5942

There is something of the Brief Encounter refreshment room about The National Café; a romantic evocation of the past in its bentwood chairs and period décor that gives it a real vintage charm. Certainly, of the many in-gallery cafes that receive the Peyton & Byrne-style treatment (restaurateur Oliver Peyton's own catering brand), The National Café is the most atmospheric, serving as a blissful retreat from Trafalgar Square.

In its relaxed, self-service tearoom you will be faced with a counter weighing heavy with plates of Peyton & Byrne classics: fluffy Chelsea buns, giant Jammie Dodger-style biscuits and a Victoria sandwich oozing sticky jam. There is a twist, however, that elevates British baking. The raspberry and coconut muffins, for example, are eye-poppingly large, with a gooey centre and sweet crusty top—far more satisfying than any choc chip. The Champagne, rhubarb and blackcurrant crumble, meanwhile, takes a mumsy desert to a new, wicked level.

The only downer is that Peyton & Byrne's own malty tea is inelegantly served in paper cups. For a more polished experience, go through to the adjoining brasserie for a cream tea with table service.

PEYTON
AND
BYRNE
Traditional Scones
Cornish clotted cream and
own Jam

Lemon Curd Tart

NATIONAL GALLERY
Café
National
Café

COCOMAYA

12 Connaught Street/3 Porchester Place, W2 2AF
www.cocomaya.co.uk
020 7706 2883

It is no surprise that Cocomaya is achingly fashionable. The brainchild of Agent Provocateur founder Serena Rees, designer Walid al Damirji and Joel Bernstein (formerly head of concept at department store Liberty), its chic atmosphere reflects its stylish owners. Part chocolatier, part bakery, Cocomaya occupies two neighbouring buildings in this classy part of town and its two large sharing tables (one in each of the premises) are routinely full. If it looks a bit of an uncomfortable squeeze, do not give up: consider a brief takeaway stop as the cakes and pastries should not be missed.

The choice is expansive and the creativity evident on the well-stacked, oversized tiered stands. It is easy to be seduced by the vanilla cheesecake, rich Devil's Food cake or one of the many fancy fruit tarts, especially those baked with creamy custard filling. The less calorific options are alluring too, so look out for the apricot, currant and pecan morning cake or simple, squidgy banana loaf. And gluten-free fanciers will love the flourless chocolate torte that features a rewarding, mousse-soft centre.

London store Postcard Teas (see pages 18–19) does the honours here, providing a good selection of loose leaf teas. If you are seated in the genteel bakery, all beech wood and marble, the Rose Bud would go well. If you are in the chocolate parlour, however, match the intense pink, green and black décor with a spiced Garam Assam Chai. A feisty complement to the sweet aroma of artisan chocolates.

THE ORIGINAL MAIDS OF HONOUR

288 Kew Road, TW9 3DU
www.theoriginalmaidsofhonour.co.uk
020 8940 2752

Several stories circulate about the origins of Maids of Honour—a sort of pastry puff with a sweet cheese curd filling—but it is widely acknowledged that they were borne from the kitchens at Hampton Court during Henry VIII's reign and became popular through his taste for them. By the mid-1700s, Richmond residents were mad about the tarts, which were being churned out by a bakery that went on to change hands, names and locations several times over the centuries. This particular Maids of Honour was opened in 1887 by the Newens family and continues to bake the pastry tarts in its antiquated tearoom. In fact, it continues to bake many quintessentially English recipes from scones and sponges to meat pies and pasties.

Its old-fashioned surrounds (and the slightly scatty service) will not be to everybody's taste, but the sitting-room style tearoom and its adjacent bakery is like a portal to the past and the sponge-like scones tangibly homemade. Just be prepared for a lack of finesse in the afternoon and cream teas, as shop-bought jam and bagged tea in stainless steel pots fail to reflect the prices. Still, tourists tend to pack this cubby-like venue (likely as part of a visit to Kew Gardens across the road) and though it is not perfect, they are rewarded with a fantastically kitsch and authentic teatime.

Original
TEAS
Maids of
RICHMOND 2752
128 KUN

MOUSE & DE LOTZ

103 Shacklewell Lane, E8 2EB
www.mousedelotz.com
020 3489 8082

Hackney may well have more than its fair share of independent cafes, but the fashionable Mouse & de Lotz is a stone's throw from the main throng of Kingsland Road and deserves making the effort to find. Yes, you will be faced with the usual mismatched furniture and floral china, but it comes with a farmhouse feel that makes it newly interesting. Vases of odd flowers and a seating area laid out like a smart country house work well with a menu that features cheese on toast with homemade chutney and loaded salt-beef bagels.

The real winner here, however, is the cafe's daily tea loaf—spread thick with butter, it is lovely with a cup of Yorkshire bagged tea. Nadya Mousawi and Victoria de Lotz, the proprietors found cheerily pottering behind the counter, like to vary their cake menu. So alongside the tea loaf, expect one gluten-free cake (such as an orange and almond), custard-smothered British classics and a special that could be an ambitious parsnip and maple syrup sponge or a decadent raspberry, white chocolate and coconut cake.

Mouse & de Lotz

Mouse & de Lotz
Bakewell Tart
£2.50

TOWPATH

Regent's Canal Towpath, between Whitmore Bridge and Kingsland Road Bridge, N1 5SB

Towpath's hideaway setting, ad hoc opening hours and complete lack of website or telephone number have done precious little to keep it off the map. The tiny, waterside cafe is a word-of-mouth hit and, on a bright day, you'll find a swarm of Londoners lounging on its alfresco furniture, watching boats and ducks bob along The Regent's Canal.

The jolly staff operate from two sheltered cubbyholes, ferrying unforgettable affogatos (super-soft, homemade ice cream, drizzled with a shot of Florentine coffee), moreish pecan butter biscuits and slices of spiced honey cake to a contented clientele. Towpath's fresh, inventive food and scenic location make for an intoxicating combination—one that reflects the style and ethos of owner and food writer Lori De Mori.

Together with inspired head chef Laura Jackson, Lori (who is also married to the wonderful photographer Jason Lowe) has a delightfully simple way with food, putting together a sweet and savoury menu that's forever exciting and always changing with the seasons. One regular highlight, however, is Towpath's house olive oil cake. Unlike most sopping oil-based cakes, this light and fluffy sponge betrays just a whisper of citrus. It is perfect breakfast fare, particularly when ordered with a mug of spicy Sri Lankan black tea sourced from Robert Wilson. Choose a dry day to try the pairing, and remember Towpath is only open during the warmer months: usually from March to October, Tuesday to Sunday, 8am until dusk.

Towpath

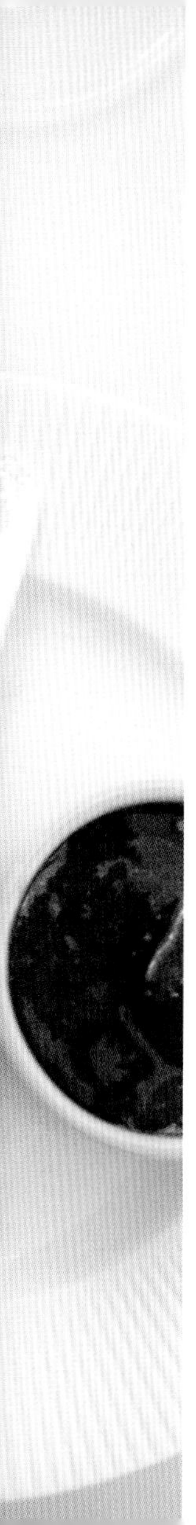

GRAND AFFAIRS

AFTERNOON TEA

When the seventh Duchess of Bedford found her spirits sinking at four o'clock, the answer was a pot of tea, light sandwiches and a little cake. That was back in 1840, and what started as a private, mid-afternoon refreshment was soon to become a popular social event. The Duchess began asking friends to join her on the lawn for tea, sparking invitations in return—by the turn of the century, afternoon tea had become a ritual among the English upper and middle classes, with crockery and etiquette developing accordingly. Hotels, too, joined suit. The Langham on Regent Street was the first to offer afternoon tea in 1865 with The Ritz following soon after. For the working classes there were tearooms where ladies, in particular, could stop for a spot of tea, a slice of cake and a natter. This grand, indulgent affair remains an institution in many upmarket London hotels, while charming tearooms have sprung up across the capital to offer a more contemporary take on tradition. This chapter features both the iconic, quintessentially English establishments as well as their modern counterparts. Elsewhere in the book, you'll find cafes and hotels serving afternoon tea with a difference, be it a gluten and dairy free option at a luxury hotel (see "Virtuous Vices") or a 1920s-themed tea served in a department store (see "Tea With a Twist").

THE RITZ

150 Piccadilly, W1J 9BR
www.theritzlondon.com
020 7300 2345

Despite its iconic familiarity, it is still easy to be impressed by The Ritz. The old-fashioned glamour of the interior, the formal civilities of the staff and its request for day guests to dress elegantly make any occasion at the hotel feel like taking a step into the past.

The afternoon tea has barely changed in decades, with the menu and the service remaining comfortingly traditional. Finger sandwiches and scones (which are markedly doughier than the norm) are topped up endlessly at your request. Cakes are generously forthcoming too, with the mini sweet numbers including a blackcurrant mousse with a white chocolate centre, a millefeuille with pear jelly and the intensely chocolaty "four chocolate Ritz cake". For a mellow accompaniment, ask for a pot of Ritz Royal English, a light-bodied blend of Assam and Ceylon. If you are lucky, long time house musician Ian Gomez will be at the keys: formerly Frank Sinatra's personal pianist, he takes requests from classical to pop, unearthing The Ritz's gentle sense of humour along the way.

Surprisingly, the event really is not as austere as you would expect. And considering that the hotel serves 400 afternoon teas a day, nor is it particularly overrun with tourists. Admittedly, you are only allowed a 95 minute sitting; and yes, you're advised to book 12 weeks in advance. But you'll leave feeling spoilt, special and, most importantly, infinitely refreshed.

THE SPATISSERIE AT THE DORCHESTER

Park Lane, W1K 1QA
www.thedorchester.com
020 7319 7109

"A little of what you love is good for you" is the motto at The Dorchester's Spatisserie, a chic, bijou annex adjoined to the hotel's spa. Cue butter-loaded finger sandwiches, warm scones and creamy bite-sized cakes: succumb to the temptation of a glass of Champagne, and this could easily be the most indulgent spa experience you will ever have.

For those with a little self-restraint, the tea menu is equally exciting, with refreshing infusions such as African Autumn (cranberry and orange) or the Organic Plum with Fresh Mint, as well as more familiar black blends.

Taking tea in The Spatisserie is a blissful way to unwind, the space overtly designed to look and feel like the epicentre of calm with feminine styling, tranquil music and soothing spa scents emanating from the treatment rooms. So while you do not need to actually book a spa treatment to enjoy the afternoon tea—and while there may not be anything inherently healthy on the cake stand—you will be left feeling thoroughly rejuvenated.

FORTNUM & MASON

181 Piccadilly, W1A 1ER
www.fortnumandmason.com
020 7734 8040

Discerning tea drinkers will perhaps find Fortnum & Mason the most enticing of London's afternoon tea destinations. An expansive list lies at the heart of the event here, some 150 single estate teas, blends and tisanes working hard to reflect the store's long, illustrious history with the beverage, one that started when royal footman William Fortnum teamed with livery stables owner Hugh Mason to become specialist grocers and tea merchants. That was back in 1707, and since then, the store has continued building on its knowledge and excellence in sourcing fine teas from around the world.

Though dense with choice, the menu is surprisingly accessible, with teas organised by strength and type and described with alluring character and drinking notes. Once you have settled on a pot, a selection of canapés signal the start of your meal, swiftly followed by a tiered stand laden with sandwiches and scones and topped with a trio of sweets: a small, spicy square of ginger parkin, a raspberry jam biscuit and a buttery Madeleine. Save room, however, as the feast is rounded off with your choice of cakes from a tray of tarts, elaborate chocolate creations, éclairs, meringues and miniature British classics. It could take a while to recover from this superior sweet and savoury fare, but the graceful, relaxed lounge of St James's Restaurant offers just the right setting and marks Fortnum & Mason as one of the best places to take afternoon tea in the capital.

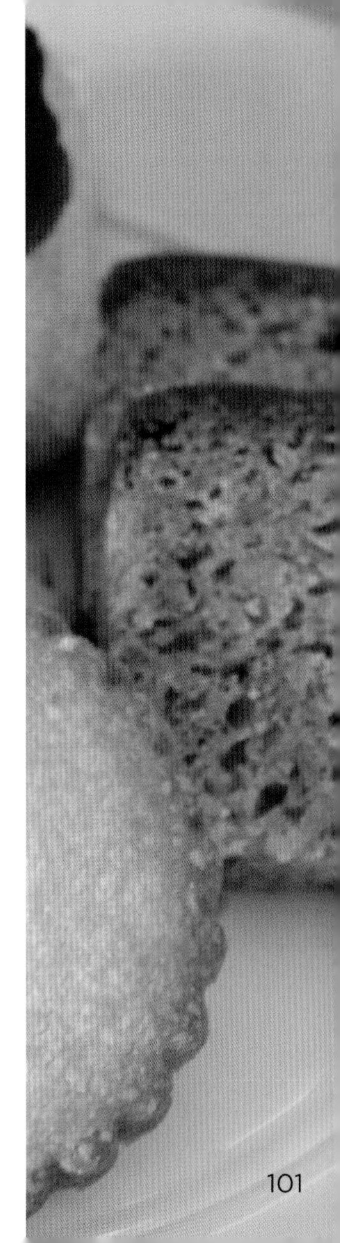

FOUNTAIN BLEND
LIGHTER TEA
FORTNUM & MASON
250g 8.8oz
LIGHT AND INFORMAL

PARIS
MAJESTIC
PARIS
POSTAGE

Fire
Exit

BOND & BROOK

63 New Bond Street, W1A 3BS
www.rhubarb.net
020 7629 0273

For ladies that lunch, Bond & Brook is a heavenly spot. Found on the light and bright third floor of department store Fenwick, it is usually buzzing with a style-conscious clientele. The décor is suitably swish: marble floors and a sculptural pewter bar hint at the cash splashed, while mid-twentieth century-inspired furniture and shelving packed with fashion books and magazines sing to the target market. Colour is thin on the ground in this predominantly white space, but the menu does a smart job of injecting a lively palette.

The afternoon tea feels like a kids' party for adults, the tone clear from the start as a dish of Smarties arrive for the table. Miniature scones and an array of tiny cakes are feminine and playful; the fondant fancies are sprinkled with gold dust and the cake stand decorated with rose petals.

The tea menu may be lacking, but prices are modest and the atmosphere and service relaxed. You would not expect any less from exacting food critic Fay Maschler and journalist Simon Davis, both consultants for this classy in-store hideaway.

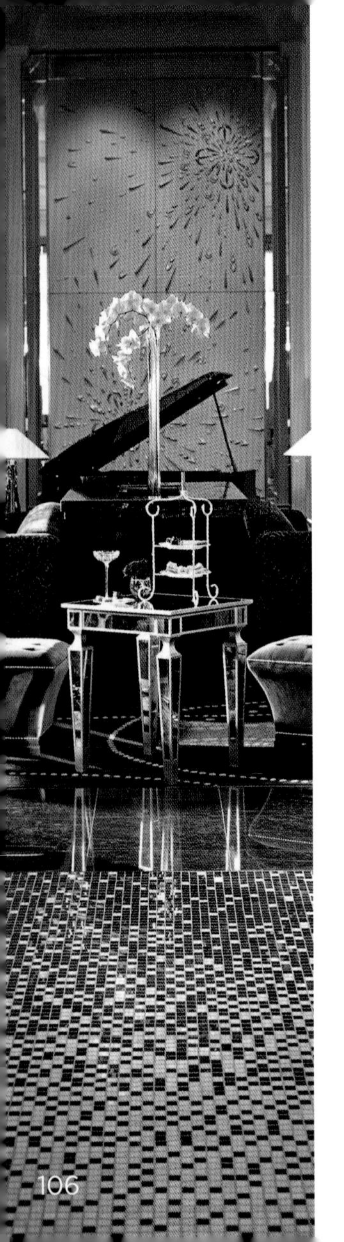

PALM COURT AT THE LANGHAM

1c Portland Place, W1B 1JA
www.palm-court.co.uk
020 7965 0195

As the first hotel in London to serve afternoon tea back in 1865, The Langham has had plenty of time to perfect its game. The central hotel continues to offer a classic experience in the grand Palm Court—a long, window-less room, tastefully decked out with glittering chandeliers, mirrored ceiling, embellished walls and low-slung lounge chairs.

The tea menu is carefully crafted by master taster Alex Probyn and features a selection of more than 35 varieties including English Tregothnan as well as Probyn's unique blends: The Langham and Palm Court. The latter is a light, rose-coloured blend of Chinese white tea, hibiscus and rosehip and is a mellow complement to Cherish Finden's spectacular cakes.

The award-winning head pastry chef riffs on The Langham's overarching fairytale theme with playful yet complex petit fours that pack multiple textures and flavours into mini portions. The traditional Wonderland Afternoon Tea brings together a good selection of these, along with a basket of warm scones and finger sandwiches. As the house pianist sets the mood, indulge in a Valrhona chocolate éclair, a rich Black Forest dome or a rosewater macaroon. Or go for the Bijoux Afternoon Tea, a show-stopping assortment of glittering cakes subtly inspired by the world's most famous jewellery houses, from Asprey to Bulgari.

ORANGE PEKOE

3 White Hart Lane, SW13 0PX
www.orangepekoeteas.com
020 8876 6070

Despite being located in the village-like Barnes, a short trek South West of London's centre, Orange Pekoe commands a devoted fan base. Its enthusiasm for loose leaf tea is a massive part of its appeal, and on each white-washed table a user-friendly booklet breaks down the source, character and even health benefits of its myriad blends, infusions and herbal drinks. Informed staff will un-lid the stacked caddies for you to see and smell the leaves, before your selection is steeped using specific water temperatures and infusion times. This attention to detail means you get an expertly brewed tea to complement your three-tiered stand loaded with generously-filled sandwiches and superlative scones.

Instead of chasing these with intricate petit fours, owners Marianna and Achilleas ask diners to choose a thick-cut slice of cake in a bid to transform the normally formal affair of afternoon tea into a more laid-back event. Options include buttery whole cakes baked on site as well as superb treats delivered from Konditor & Cook (see pages 128–131). The rustic selection marks out Orange Pekoe as a quality and cosy alternative to high-end hotel offerings.

ORANGE PEKOE
FORMOSA OOLONG
ORANGE PEKOE
FORMOSA OOLONG EXCELSIOR
ORANGE PEKOE
LAPSANG SOUCHONG
ORANGE PEKOE
CHINA OOLONG TIT KON YUM
ORANGE PEKOE
WINTER
ORANGE PEKOE
ROSE POUCHONG
ORANGE PEKOE
ALMOND

ORANGE PEKOE
LANE

THE SAVOY

Strand, WC2R 0EU
www.fairmont.com
020 7420 2111

Following a staggeringly expensive restoration, The Savoy is every bit the grand English hotel. Founded by impresario Richard D'Oyly Carte as London's first luxury hotel in 1889, The Savoy remains evocative of its glamorous past. At its centre lies the Thames Foyer, a fine lounge where the prettiest elements of the hotel's Edwardian and Art Deco design meet. Here, a majestic ceiling dome with stained glass looks down over a birdcage-style gazebo housing a grand piano and pianist. It is a fairytale setting, and a dreamy place to take a very ceremonial afternoon tea.

Without making you feel like a tourist, enthusiastic staff ferry out sandwiches and scones with old-fashioned politeness, before the floral Wedgwood china is filled with French pastries of your choosing (opt for the chocolate and pistachio Opera, a good twist on a classic) followed swiftly by proper British bakes that include a somewhat citrus-heavy English fruitcake. As the cakes come thick and fast, waiting staff encourage you to try several different pots of tea during your sitting, taking you through a substantial list of familiar black teas, scented blends and tisanes.

Chances are, you will go on to buy a caddy of loose leaves at the new Savoy Tea—a petite in-house store where, if you cannot commit to a full afternoon tea, you can also buy single versions of those French pastries or divine artisan chocolates.

TEA

BEA'S OF BLOOMSBURY

44 Theobald's Road, WC1X 8NW
www.beasofbloomsbury.com
020 7242 8330

Bea Vo likes to do teatime a little differently—and her personality is all over this bustling Bloomsbury tearoom. Vo, formerly a pastry chef at Nobu and Asia de Cuba relies on natural, top quality ingredients for her cakes and bakes them with her American roots in mind. There is bourbon in the apple loaf and as well as a sinfully good rocky road—and the afternoon tea comes US-style too. For this, scones are baked for longer and on a lower temperature than usual so they become crumbly rather than doughy, just how they like them Stateside. These fragile treats join fudgy bite-sized brownies and blondies; a meringue topped marshmallow; and classic, soft-iced cupcakes on a simple tiered stand.

The weekend sees afternoon teas book up fast, but for the impulsive there are always plenty of cakes piled high and wide in glass cabinets with an ogling queue to boot. If it really is too busy to wedge your way in, look out for Bea's of Bloomsbury's pop-up stalls at festivals and food events, or head to the more polished branch in the One New Change shopping centre at St Paul's.

CLARIDGE'S

Brook Street, W1K 4HR
www.claridges.co.uk
020 7629 8860

The Foyer dining space at Claridge's may be a bit old hat, but there is no denying it's a handsome place in which to take tea. Its gentle lighting and green, cream and gold colour scheme lend it a traditional warmth, while at its centre, a contemporary, blown glass sculpture by Dale Chihuly hangs from the high ceiling.

Service is enthusiastic rather than smothering, and the waiting staff can confidently recommend one of the 30 teas on the menu. Here, Marco Polo is the unquestionable star. Imported from French tea salon Mariage Frères, the smooth black blend is spiced with Chinese and Tibetan fruits and flowers, giving it a naturally sweet, aromatic flavour. The tea also forms the basis of the Marco Polo jelly, which, after a glut of fluffy triangular sandwiches, is served with scones and clotted cream. In the world of classic afternoon teas, this enlivening jelly is a bold departure from strawberry jam—and one that pays off. The following French confections, however, aren't quite as adventurous. The selection changes with brisk frequency, but tends to cover the familiar, be it a delicate fruit tart or raspberry and rosewater macaroon, and is always sensationally executed.

ORANGERY

Kensington Palace, Kensington Gardens, W8 4PX
www.hrp.org.uk
020 3166 6113

The Orangery is almost all about location. The grand building—formerly Queen Anne's lavish greenhouse and alfresco dining entertainment space—is part of Kensington Palace's grounds and as such, looks out on to pristine palatial lawns. In summer, the sun-kissed veranda is full of tourists-in-the-know and Kensington locals enjoying brunch, lunch or afternoon tea under white parasols. Inside, a central table hosts a mountain of scones together with whole cakes and tarts that look good enough to distract you from the Orangery itself—a long, sunlit pavilion with oversized windows, Corinthian columns and a real sense of regal charm.

The Signature Orange Tea is served with minimal flash or ceremony, the finger sandwiches, orange scones, and orange-themed tart and creamy chocolate éclair arriving together on white china. The scented scones are actually fairly potent in flavour, so avoid pairing this afternoon tea with the recommended Rooibos breakfast (also with citrus notes) and try one of the black Tregothnan teas instead. Sourced from a family-run estate in Cornwall, the Tregothnan blends offer a rare chance to taste British-grown tea and support the sustainability of the estate.

THE PARLOUR AT SKETCH

9 Conduit Street, W1S 2XG
www.sketch.uk.com
020 7659 4500

Well-known for its two flamboyant restaurants and bonkers interiors, Sketch has become an eccentric London institution. Tea is served in its third space, The Parlour, where antique chairs upholstered in eclectic fabrics meet lively avant-garde art and outrageous light fittings. What is pleasing about teatime here, is that no two visits are alike. Founders Mourad Mazouz and Pierre Gagnaire have done a sensational job of avoiding the style-over-substance cliché, and continue to encourage evolution in the design and menu. Mazouz particularly loves to tinker with the furnishings, removing a chair here, re-covering one there, while pastry chef Damien Piscioneri looks to experiment with flavours and textures.

Cakes vie for attention from a showcase cabinet and the selection is a delight. Caramel éclairs, perfectly turned out canelés, nut-packed brownies, Mont Blancs and a decadent guanaja cake layered skillfully with hazelnut, praline and Sacher biscuit all feature. Served on vintage floral crockery, afternoon tea brings together a choice of sweet fancies with finger sandwiches and warm scones, and its best enjoyed with tea specialist Jing's Yunnan Gold—a honey-like, malty blend that fits well with the fare.

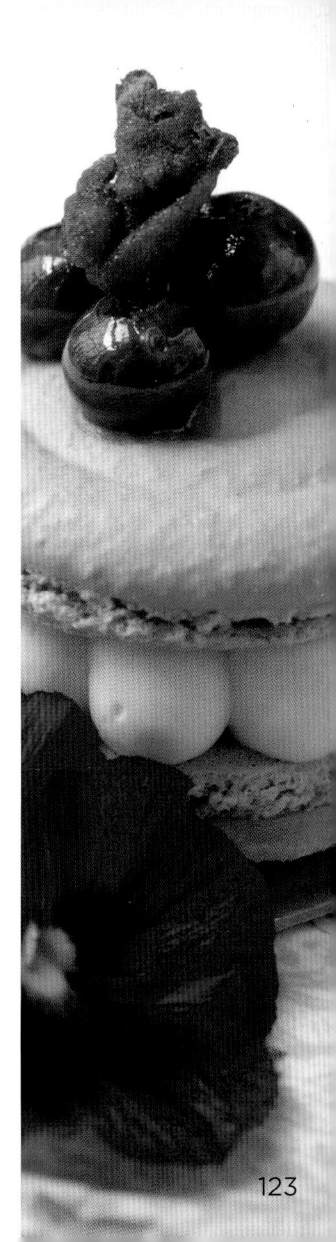

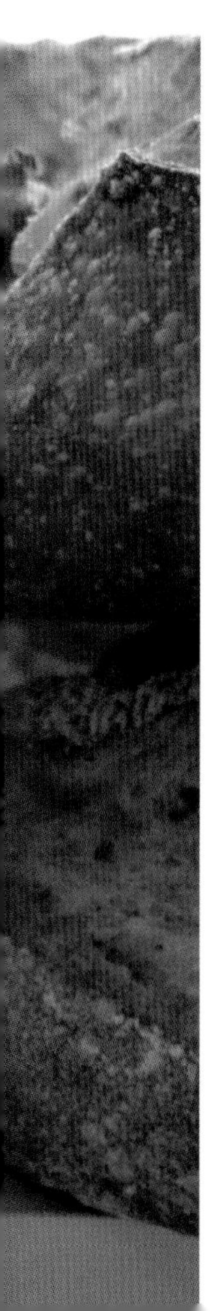

POP IN, TAKE OUT

BAKERIES & PATISSERIES

There is something intrinsically satisfying about home baking. The moment the oven alarm bell sounds and you are able to pull out a perfectly bouncy sponge or hand-cut biscuits, you get a thrill that is hard to beat. But, despite our best intentions and a prevalent dedication to hoarding cookery books, home baking is not always possible. In reality, the time, energy and expense of starting a recipe from scratch can mean the kitchen gets overlooked, while the odd baking disaster can stall our willingness to get back into that apron. It is wonderful, then, that there is a sweet-fix safety net.

Quality bakeries and patisseries across London are packed with bakers happily dedicated to supplying city folk with hearty cakes, buns and pastries. "Pop In, Take Out" brings you the best of these, covering one-off, local independents as well as growing mini chains. It focuses on those comforting stops where you can drop in for a quick snack or pick up an array of fancies to take back home to your own tea party.

BELLE EPOQUE

37 Newington Green, N16 9PR
www.belleepoque.co.uk
020 7249 2222

Inspired by the golden age of European history prior to the First World War, and the master craftsmen that helped characterise the period, Eric and Hulya Rousseau look to honour the artisan traditions of French patisserie in their always-lively Newington Green cafe. The pair source almost all of their raw ingredients from their home country, and pâtissier Eric and his tight-knit staff make everything from scratch.

Froufrou French pastries include a tangibly fresh Fraisier with a pink marzipan topping; and an ultra-flashy Meridien with a mouth-filling vanilla pannacotta and chocolate mousse centre. Despite the presence of these fancies (together with handmade chocolates and macaroons), the patisserie itself has a rustic appeal, painted in classic Provençal pastel colours and starring a romantic alfresco garden. It is a look that matches Belle Epoque's cheering, billowing viennoiseries (try the superior pain aux chocolat), and its many excellent country-style tarts. You can also sample the patisserie's creations at 1920s tearoom Dolly's (see pages 164–165) based in Selfridges.

Petits Cœurs
MIKADO
MIKADO
LANGUE DE CHAT
TUILES AMANDES
Figolu

KONDITOR & COOK

22 Cornwall Road, SE1 8TW
www.konditorandcook.com
020 7261 0456

Gerhard Jenne cottoned onto the appeal of fresh baking and quality, organic ingredients long before both became fashionable. The German pastry chef (or konditor) opened his first artisan bakery back in 1993, making use of a Victorian shop on a quiet Waterloo side street. Cornwall Road is now firmly on the foodie map and the original store (now one of a handful of outlets across London) remains popular.

Its period-looking interior is almost as irresistible as the cakes arranged along the shop's purple windowsills. From the Konditor & Cook signature classics, you would do well to go for the renowned Curly Whirly with its dark chocolate sponge and cheese-based vanilla frosting. Alternatively, the rich Whiskey Bomb has a real kick, and the trademark brownies are baked for those who like them dense and gooey. Jenne's reputation for unusual or humorously iced celebration cakes has also become something of a calling card. His Magic Cakes, too, have won a legion of fans, though the small, fondant squares with varying novelty icing are not a patch on the bakery's more grown-up creations.

ALMOND
FRUIT TART
ALMOND
ST CLEMENT
ALMOND
FRUIT TART

Konditor & Cook

PECAN PIE
GAIL's
BROWNIE FINGER
GAIL's

GAIL'S

138 Portobello Road, W11 2DZ
www.gailsbread.co.uk
020 7460 0766

Be it Melrose and Morgan, Daylesford Organic or Ottolenghi, London undeniably does a fine line in smart deli-bakery crossovers. Gail's, however, gets a special mention by virtue of putting the baking first. The founding Hampstead branch was opened in 2005 by former management consultants Ran Avidan and Tom Molnar who left their jobs to pursue an alternative career in baking and learnt their trade by working with Gail Mejia—the expert talent behind wholesale bakery The Bread Factory and the original founder of Baker & Spice. Though this enterprise does not directly involve Mejia, her name appears to bring good luck, as Gail's has gone from strength to strength, opening close to a dozen branches across the capital.

This lovely Notting Hill outlet stars abundant cafe seating, serves Jing teas and Union coffee, and gives away its owners' real obsession with bread, as well as internationally-inspired pastries and cakes. The emphasis is on individually turned-out tarts, slices and fondants rather than heavyweight sponges, so make a beeline for the chocolate pecan brownies, dense and fruit-heavy apple squares or the mini maple raisin fingers. Gail's prides itself on making everything with natural ingredients and without added preservatives, artificial colourings or flavourings. It may mean the prices are a little on the steep side, but for a one-off tea and cake treat, it merits the extra pennies.

GAIL's

PASSON FRUIT
COOKIE
OUT: 2.25 IN: 2.70
GAIL's

CLARKE'S

122 Kensington Church Street, W8 4BH
www.sallyclarke.com
020 7229 2190

After more than 25 years of successful business, it is surprising that Clarke's hasn't turned into a chain. This is by no means due to a lack of popularity—Sally Clarke MBE has ensured her establishment's reputation is nothing short of impeccable—rather it is because of a simple belief in quality over quantity. By remaining a relatively small business, Sally can continue to manage Clarke's restaurant (where the menu changes twice daily), the wholesale bakery (which turns out some 2,000 loaves a day) and the always bustling shop that stocks homemade jams, chutneys and sauces.

The shop also houses glass counters full of baked goods, from breads and pastries to tarts and quiches. If you are in a decadent mood, point straight to the luscious dark chocolate and almond cake; if it is an everyday sweet fix you are after, the carrot and walnut cake with orange zest in the cream cheese frosting is moist, moreish and justifies crossing town for. In truth, it is hard to go wrong in Clarke's. Everything is made with such love, and using such fresh ingredients, that whatever you choose will have the sweet taste of superlative home baking.

Hot
Cross
Bun
£1.30

THE HUMMINGBIRD BAKERY

133 Portobello Road, W11 2DY
www.hummingbirdbakery.com
020 7851 1795

For many, The Hummingbird Bakery needs precious little introduction. Tarek Malouf, a Brit in love with American baking, opened the Portobello Road bakery back in 2004 and is often credited as the man who introduced Londoners to the now much-loved Red Velvet cake and fuelled our passion for frosted cupcakes. Celebrities rated his style, helping Hummingbird expand into a brand with further outposts in South Kensington, Soho and Spitalfields, as well as a bestselling cookbook that reaches out to cake-lovers beyond the capital.

Pop into the original West London branch, wait patiently in a line of tourists, and you will be rewarded with tooth-achingly sweet inventions that are still worth talking about. Look out for the Devil's Food cake or extravagant Black Bottom cupcake with its chocolate sponge, cheesecake centre and cream cheese frosting. There is only a small bar to sit at inside, so instead, wander down the iconic Portobello Road with a decadently-filled whoopee pie, a slab of rocky road or an iced creation in hand.

PAUL RHODES BAKERY

37 King William Walk, SE10 9HU
www.paulrhodeslondon.co.uk
020 8269 0460

The multi Michelin-star chef Paul Rhodes has worked in some of the classiest kitchens in town. Starting under Pierre Koffman in La Tante Claire, he went on to work at a string of top-end restaurants. In fact, he spent more than 15 years in whites before he finally succumbed to his true passion: baking. In 2003, he set up a wholesale enterprise with the idea of supplying London restaurants and hotels with pastries and breads straight from the oven. By 2008, he had opened his first high street bakery. Now a thriving business in the heart of South London's tourist hotspot, Greenwich, Paul Rhodes is testament to the appeal of good baking.

The loaves—plain bloomers, soda, sour dough, focaccia—are uniformly and supremely good. The cakes and pastries are a cut above. A very British thread runs through them and the shortbread, Bakewell tarts, Chelsea buns and apple cake are all traditionally turned out. Do not overlook the thick, fudgy brownies or the sweet American cookies, though, and pop in regularly for seasonal specials from well-filled mince pies to ghoulish Halloween cakes. The Greenwich branch is great for a quick takeaway, while the more spacious Notting Hill branch offers the chance to sit in.

PAUL

RHODES
Lemon Tart
£2.80

BLACKBIRD BAKERY

378 Norwood Road, SE27 9AA
020 8670 5874

From modest beginnings, Eammon Sweeny has built Blackbird Bakery into something of an empire over in South East London. He started as a wholesale supplier but, following a trial stall in North Cross Road Market, he found there was a strong local demand for his breads and cakes. The first Blackbird Bakery (a tiny shop in Herne Hill) soon followed and the brand has continued to expand.

For inspiration, Sweeny continues to draw on his time as a baker in the US, where he learnt his trade at the well-regarded Black Dog Bakery on Martha's Vineyard. His cakes have an understated American influence: this is not cupcake territory, rather here you will find a booze-loaded pecan and whiskey tart, and batches of homemade pancake mixture for sale in takeaway boxes. There is a place to perch in all the stores, and each has a different character with reclaimed furniture (an old pub bar serves as a counter in the Norwood Road branch) and jolly black and yellow colour scheme. This is a homely, local bakery: always well stocked, always busy and just the kind of independent-spirited place you would be happy to see spring up on every high street.

OTTOLENGHI

OTTOLENGHI

63 Ledbury Road, W11 2AD
www.ottolenghi.co.uk
020 7727 1121

White lacquer dominates the sleek outlets of Ottolenghi: this is no cosy deli-bakery. In fact, the minimalist design is so fashionably spartan it might easily discourage less-stylish clientele at the threshold. That is, if it were not for the seductive display of tarts, cakes, pastries, salads and breads peering out from the window. This heartening collection changes daily and literally lures you in from the street. Who could resist a macadamia and almond cheesecake, a buttermilk scone with orange peel, or a passion fruit meringue tart?

Founders Yotam Ottolenghi (who originally worked for Baker & Spice) and business partner Noam Bar have seen the popularity of their venture explode exponentially since the first takeaway opened off Westbourne Grove in 2002, the brand's acclaimed cookbooks doing much to broaden its appeal. Chef Sami Tamimi designs the menu, taking influences from Mediterranean, Middle Eastern and British cuisine, whilst using largely organic ingredients sourced from the UK. Despite a new brasserie in Soho, the cakes are still best enjoyed at one of the smaller, local takeaway shops such as this.

LOVE BAKERY

319 King's Road, SW3 5EP
www.lovebakery.co.uk
020 7352 3191

The day that Samantha Blears took a tray of her homemade cupcakes to the school fête was the day her new career was born. Children and parents went wild for her mini cakes and soon Blears was baking them by the dozen for parties and events. Before long, she was confident enough to open up a small bakery on the King's Road.

In complete contrast to the locale's usually slick appearance, Love Bakery is a lively cupcake boutique, packed with character and manned by super-friendly staff. The cakes are still homemade—the kitchen even relies on domestic mixers, ovens and utensils rather than industrial equipment—and the result is fluffy sponges and creamy toppings that look and taste exactly like ones you might buy from a mum at a fair. Flavours can be leftfield—be prepared for rhubarb and ginger, raspberry and coconut, or even elderflower among the more familiar staples—and lower than average prices reflect Blears' laid-back attitude toward the whole enterprise. As she puts it "it is, after all, just cake".

PIZZA & FOCACCIA
HOT FOOD
SALADS
TEA & COFFEE
BEVERAGES
CHOCOLATE SLICE
CHOCOLATE & TOFFEE
CAPRESE

PRINCI

135 Wardour Street, W1F 0UT
www.princi.co.uk
020 7478 8888

When Alan Yau, the restaurateur behind Hakkasan and Wagamama, took a fancy to Milan's already established bakery-cum-eatery Princi, London was in for a treat. Yau teamed up with master Italian bread baker Rocco Princi and opened Soho's first branch in 2008, signalling new competition for the equally polished French chains Paul and Patisserie Valerie.

Breads, pastries, cakes, pizza slices and salads are lined up attractively in a long counter, while in the background, bakers slide warm bread from a wood-fired oven. You might question its authenticity if it were not for the sound of Italians ordering loaves by the dozen. It has proved a hit with London locals too, its long sharing tables and bar-like perches busy—sometimes right up until the midnight closing time.

Ordering can be tricky, with no obvious queue and different stations at which to collect drinks and food, but the culinary standard makes up for this. Viennoiseries are outstandingly good and the choice is broad, taking in custard-filled cannoncini and mini croissants with a dollop of raspberry jam. Cakes tend to be heavy (there's a very satisfying pear and apple slice) and act as a counterpoint to mini options such as hard almond kisses, milk buns and sweet, soft Madeleines. These are ideal for taking out and nibbling while you walk. Though there is also plenty of space to sit in and admire Princi's conscious attempt to unite water, wind and fire—apparently vital elements in baking—with a 19 metre long water feature, with brass and limestone fittings.

LISBOA PATISSERIE

57 Golborne Road, W10 5NR
020 8968 5242

Locals often pack out this Portuguese patisserie so come prepared to hustle for a seat and be served brusquely by the friendly, efficient staff. They are used to keeping the queue moving, so to avoid lengthy deliberation, point to the flaky and buttery pastéis de nata (custard tarts) or the pastéis de coco (the coconut version) for two failsafe options.

Elsewhere, the counter is heaving with largely egg and sugar-based pastries and cakes; Portuguese customers clamour over these, so you might have to battle for your bag of palmiers (palm-shaped butter biscuits), pão de leites (milk bread rolls) or bolas de Berlim (the regional take on Germany's Berliners).

If there is a seat among the chattering regulars and Portobello Market shoppers, try the Sical coffee served in tall glasses or a strong espresso, Iberian style. Look to the other side of the road for the Lisboa Delicatessen, which is well stocked with Portuguese meats, salt cod and larder essentials. Further Lisboa patisserie-deli branches can be found in Camden, Chelsea and Stockwell.

Lisboa-London

TEA WITH A TWIST

ALTERNATIVE & THEMED

Although every entry in this book is unique in some way, "Tea With a Twist" is about acknowledging those that look to offer a one-off experience. It celebrates the city's best alternative thinkers, and shows off an eccentric culture that works in counterpoint to London's glut of chain cafes. They even stand in contrast to the best independents by creating themed or alternative settings that turn the familiar joy of taking tea into something extraordinary. Alongside leftfield cafes, this chapter also highlights places that offer their own interpretation of a traditional British teatime (the Arabic afternoon tea at Mo Café, for instance), or introduce a completely foreign teatime ceremony (such as the Hungarian Louis Patisserie). The selection not only reflects London's love of the unconventional, but also its inhabitants' eagerness to try something new.

THE SANDERSON

50 Berners Street, W1T 3NG
www.sandersonlondon.com
020 7300 1400

Philippe Starck designed The Sanderson's interior with *Alice's Adventures In Wonderland* in mind, making the hotel the perfect setting for the aptly-billed Mad Hatter's Afternoon Tea. Aim for a summer visit when tea is served in the lush courtyard rather than the plain Suka restaurant, and get ready for a fancy fusion of Lewis Caroll's and Starck's unique vision.

Presented on teacup-topped cake stand, the meal kicks off with multi-coloured finger sandwiches made from mild-flavoured saffron, spinach and beetroot breads, before it takes a turn toward tradition with a couple of crumbly scones. Oddball invention is saved for the sweet tier, the highlight here being an enjoyable brown bottle with a "drink me" tag hanging from its neck. Suck slowly on the mini straw and you will take in a trio of liquid layers that taste just like apple pie, lemon curd and English toffee. The stand is topped with a pair of lollies—one blueberry number that magically turns your mouth from hot to cold, and an exploding chocolate pop with an ice-cream centre. It is all terribly novel and a lot of fun, even if the accompanying bagged tea is disappointing. Technically, this may not be the best quality afternoon tea in London, but you will be hard pushed to find one with such an abundance of pleasing and playful charm.

Drink me

Drink me

VANILLI'S

Red
Velvet
£3

Berry Jam
Donughts
with vanilla
sugar
£2

LILY VANILLI BAKERY

6 The Courtyard, Ezra Street, E2 7RG
www.lilyvanilli.com
No telephone

Open only on Sundays, this dinky little East End bakery is usually packed with shoppers spilling over from Columbia Road and its weekly flower market. Adventurous cake eaters are routinely among the pack, rooting out Lily 'Vanilli' Jones's experimental treats, from roasted grapefruit and almond tart to delicately spiced-plum doughnuts and a wicked absinthe and mint choc chip ice cream.

Those familiar with the baker's work might be surprised by the lack of gore (Lily made her name creating sculptural and macabre sweet creations including ultra-realistic beating heart cakes), but the fare focuses on unusual flavour combinations rather than novelty bakes. Vanilli is constantly pushing the limits in the kitchen, and though she whips up alternative treats with aplomb, she is also a dab hand at the crowd-pleasers. Bakewells, vanilla cupcakes and gooey chocolate brownies are staples, as well as savouries such as rustic sausage rolls and elegant veg tarts. You'll also always be sure of a good cup of Coleman coffee (a London-based roaster) or a cup of Clipper tea. Be prepared to take away though, as the cosy cafe has limited indoor and outdoor seating.

SANCTUM SOHO

20 Warwick Street, W1B 5NF
www.sanctumsoho.com
020 7292 6102

There are no finger sandwiches, no scones and certainly no petit fours at Sanctum Soho's somewhat pricey Gentleman's Afternoon Tea. Instead, meat rules supreme. The hors d'œuvres give men (or brave women) the chance to sink their teeth into seared steak on sourdough, and tackle a poached oyster with a piquant Bloody Mary relish. In place of those dainty teatime sandwiches, expect miniature versions of British mains including a lamb and potato hotpot with a deliciously cheesy crust and a dinky Yorkshire pudding with roast beef and horseradish. Served on slate boards in the dimly lit, masculine surrounds of the hotel's No. 20 restaurant, this is indeed a manly affair. For afters, those with a sweet-tooth can dig into a slice of dense chocolate fudge cake before the afternoon tea takes a rock'n'roll turn. Guests are poured a serving of Jack Daniel's whiskey in tankards—a Single Barrel, Gentleman Jack or the original Old No. 7—offered a cigar and led to the roof garden to kick back in the outdoor lounge. You will get a sense of Sanctum Soho's more decadent credentials here, perhaps catching guests frolicking in the alfresco hot tub, or finding yourself reveling with famous faces until the early hours.

LOUIS PATISSERIE

32 Heath Street, NW3 6TE
020 7435 9908

Hungarians differ in their opinion as to whether Louis Patisserie is truly representative of their country's cakes and patisserie, though the debate need not cloud your visit—this Hampstead gem is almost all about the experience. Brown wooden panels, tan leather booth seating and wooden furniture create a formal, old-world ambiance, while the traditional service completes the ceremony. If you ask for cake, a waitress will promptly bring out an over-sized tray crowded with mostly cream-loaded slices. She will talk you through the Hungarian classics, the French staples and even a few Polish additions. Tea (only the English breakfast is loose) is then served in silverware and poured into dainty porcelain teacups. All the while, you will hear intellectual types musing philosophically, and see lone cake-eaters reading intently. The dobosh (an iconic Hungarian cake made from layers of sponge, buttercream and caramel) may be on the dry side, but this is a great spot to people watch, and a novel way to take tea.

DRINK, SHOP & DO

9 Caledonian Road, N1 9DX
www.drinkshopdo.com
020 3343 9138

When old school friends Kristie and Coralie decided to bring together their many interests and open a pop up shop that combined tea, cake, retro furniture and crafty hobbies, little did they anticipate the positive response. Not least because of the rather drab Caledonian Road location. Happily, the trial was a success and the pair decided to permanently occupy the King's Cross space, turning a former Victorian bathhouse into a colourful cafe and bar.

Always buzzing, Drink, Shop & Do is a charismatic amalgamation of its owners' interests. The tea menu is put together by Kristie, who gently guides tea newcomers toward new and unique loose leaf blends. And Coralie is always on the hunt for interesting crafts to stock in their little boutique. As with the constantly changing furniture (all the reclaimed tables and chairs are for sale), the cakes change every week and the selection of fruit-loaded sponges and British bakes always reflect the seasons. Come evening, cakes are replaced with cocktails and the venue lives up to the final part of its name by hosting a serious of oddball practical events such as Knit Night, Play With Clay or paper plane-making evening, Fold & Fly.

DOLLY'S CAFE

Selfridges, 400 Oxford Street, W1A 1AB
www.selfridges.com
020 7318 3616

The Hungarian-born Dolly Sisters made their name on the American vaudeville circuit, joining Ziegfeld Follies in 1911 and dancing their way into the 1920s. But it was not until they met Harry Gordon Selfridge that their personal lives became as famous as their stage name. The businessman found much to admire in the fun-loving Dolly Sisters, embroiling himself in scandal as he embarked on a love affair with the twins. Today, department store Selfridges celebrates its founder's frivolous mischief in this refined, themed tearoom. Dolly's reflects the showgirls' alluring persona through original art deco teapots, bespoke silver cutlery, marble flooring and luxury fittings.

Though glamorous, the finish barely distracts from the fact that the tearoom sits exposed at the centre of a homeware department and is surrounded by shoppers. If you like people watching, this is no great shortcoming; though the atmosphere can feel clamorous. Cakes crafted by Eric Rousseau and his Belle Epoque patisserie (see pages 126–127) are a successful diversion, as are the wondrous Petit Pois by Harry Eastwood and Ashley Maddox—gluten and wheat-free cupcakes in which butter is replaced with courgette, pumpkin or beetroot. Both goodies can be ordered separately, though you can also take your time over a Dolly's cream or afternoon tea, together with a pot of Selfridges' own range of fine teas.

MO CAFÉ

25 Heddon Street, W1B 4BH
www.momoresto.com
020 7434 4040

Though situated directly next door to its older sibling (the deluxe Arabic restaurant Momo), Mo Café has forsaken its elder's glamour in favour of a traditional souk tearoom-look with hanging lanterns, low cushioned seating and metal tray topped tables. The intimate space is totally in keeping with Parisian-Algerian restaurateur Mourad Mazouz's unique style and it is where you can try a so-called Moroccan afternoon tea.

The fare itself rarely matches the authenticity of its surroundings, instead fusing the best bits of British teatime with Arabic accents. Moroccan chicken wraps, for example, are among the sandwiches; the scones come with strawberry and fig jam; and a honey-sweet Crêpes Berber joins a fruit-topped cheesecake. The coriander in the chocolate delice may be barely detectable, but this is forgiven on sight of the twinkling selection of Maghrebine pastries. These North African delicacies are reliant on the thick, sugary almond paste so popular in the region and are not for the health-conscious—nor is the syrupy mint tea. For something less toothache-inducing, pair the sweets with a pot of the Turkish Hammam which blends orange flower water and rose petals with a robust green tea base.

THE BERKELEY

Wilton Place, SW1X 7RL
www.the-berkeley.co.uk
020 7107 8866

Marrying food and fashion, Prêt-à-Porter at The Berkeley is presented as the "fashionista's afternoon tea". Fittingly, every detail is geared toward the stylish, from the Paul Smith-designed china, to the waitresses in one-off taffeta dresses. On the cake stand couture creations vary to take the shape of a handbag, dress, or simply encapsulate the attitude of a designer in an abstract form.

The hotel's head pastry chef Mourad Khiat designs the cutting-edge confections, and with one eye on the latest catwalk trends, updates them with the seasons taking inspiration from designers such as Anya Hindmarch, Christian Louboutin, Alexander McQueen and Marc Jacobs. Surprisingly for novelty fare, the cakes and biscuits are actually exquisite to eat, all rich chocolate sponges, delicate fruit mousses and interesting accent flavours from cassis to lychee. There are no scones to break up the sugary line-up, but there are two savoury plates, one of finger sandwiches, another of chichi canapés such as seared tuna on a spoon or a shot of chilled soup.

Real darlings of the fashion world will want to team the meal with Laurent-Perrier Champagne, though a pot of the black Berkeley Blend is a warming accompaniment, while the fragrant White Peony would make a refreshing contrast to all the sugar.

VANILLA & CREAM
HONEY & ALMOND
london bus
biscuit tin
Little Devils

YOU DON'T BRING ME FLOWERS

15 Staplehurst Road, SE13 5ND
www.youdontbringmeflowers.co.uk
020 8297 2333

The scent of freshly cut blooms greets you warmly at the door of this enchanting cafe-cum-florist. Boxes and buckets filled with stems and pot plants decorate the shop outside and fill half the space indoors. The other half is given over to a ramshackle cafe workstation behind which retro crockery is stacked higgledy-piggledy and aproned ladies busily prepare pots of tea and cut healthy slices of homemade cake. It is utterly twee, totally genuine and every bit as picturesque as it sounds.

Lynne Norledge runs the shop, serving cakes made locally by friends, as well as a savoury menu of soups and sandwiches. She opened the shop in response to the dearth of characterful services in Lewisham's sleepy Hither Green and has made You Don't Bring Me Flowers one of the only reasons to visit the area. Of course, locals will hate to have their prized secret unveiled, but this gorgeous spot is hard to keep under wraps, and easily justifies the 15 minute train journey south from London Bridge. Ask for a pot of tea, slice of tart rhubarb and stem ginger cake (or the punchy double espresso and walnut sponge) and head to the living-room style seating upstairs or the tiny terrace decked with flowers.

AFTERNOON TEASE AT VOLUPTÉ

9 Norwich Street, EC4A 1EJ
www.timefortease.co.uk
020 7831 1622

From the outside, you will think you are in the wrong place. But that is the beauty of the well-concealed Volupté—it makes you feel like you are rooting out a retro den of decadence, where the cocktails are poured hard and fast and burlesque entertainment is at its illicit best. The thrill appears to be popular with hen parties and vintage-minded couples, both of which are in major attendance when Zoe Fletcher presents her Afternoon Tease several times a month in the basement venue. The event brings together the best sultry cabaret acts with a pot of proper loose leaf tea, sandwiches and cakes. Much imitated, this marriage of tea and burlesque is now on offer at various venues in London, though Afternoon Tease is the original and the best.

Still, with only a brief assortment of sweet treats and slightly miserly sandwich fillings, it is safe to stress that you will not be getting a first-class afternoon tea in terms of cuisine here at Volupté. What you will get is a superior alternative experience. Zoe certainly has an eye for a coquettish star, presenting Polly Rae before she became a West End name and booking sterling acts including Amber Topaz and Vicky Butterfly. As with most burlesque, the entertainment is innocent enough, taking first-timers gently into a world of cheeky comedy, saucy titillation and gorgeous glamour—only here, it comes with a teatime twist.

V

Food
Brekkie
Sandwiches (Wholemeal, White or Bagel)
Ploughmans (w Ham +50p)
Feta, Olive Tapenade w Rocket
Goats Cheese, Tomato w Spinach
Roast Rare Beef, Horseradish, Tomato
Salads
Artichoke, Tomato & Ham
Loose Teas
Green Tea
Jasmine Tea
Chamomile Flowers
Peppermint
Earl Grey
Apple & Cinnamon

CAFE VINTAGE

88 Mountgrove Road, N5 2LT
www.cafevintage.co.uk

Nothing adds to the joy of shopping like a spot of tea and cake, which is why Cafe Vintage is such a darling idea. Sisters Aysha Sparks and Nadia Allman opened this clothes boutique and tearoom with British wartime in mind, and both the secondhand threads and homemade cakes are obviously nostalgic. So while Aysha is busy rooting out items for the eclectic shop, Nadia looks after most of the baking, drawing on old English recipes to set her cakes apart. There is beetroot in the chocolate sponge (a trick originally used to help the sugar ration go further) and a hardy date and walnut loaf among simple, iced fairy cakes and a grandiose Victoria sandwich. She also buys in artisan muffins and fluffy hazelnut and raisin bread that is served toasted and smothered in jam. The drinks are traditional too; the pair have sourced a beautifully light Earl Grey with obvious citrus character from Williamson Tea, and present it by the pot along with loose blends from the excellent Edinburgh based specialist, PekoeTea.

The owners' DIY effort with reclaimed tables and decorative knick-knacks gives the sunny, south-facing store an inviting feel and its location—tucked away on an unassuming side street—also has its appeals. Just a few doors down you will find a bespoke cycle workshop, antique store, a contemporary gallery, and a shop dedicated to selling Sylvanian Families. Cafe Vintage's place among this cluster of independents means Mountgrove Road is slowly becoming a worthy destination.

VIRTUOUS VICES

VEGAN & ALLERGY-FRIENDLY

If veganism, food allergies or intolerances have caused you to swear off confections (or resort to artificially-modified alternatives), then the steady growth in the number of specialist cafes and cake shops in London should come as pleasing news. There has also been a welcome surge in the number of everyday cafes and upmarket tearooms adding vegan, gluten-free, wheat-free or sugar-free cakes to their menus.

While many entries in this book look to make a point of these, "Virtuous Vices" is a chapter dedicated to places that cater comprehensively for specialist diets. Home baking and honest ingredients are key in this selection, and although some of the inclusions are all-purpose eateries rather than cafes designed solely with cake in mind, all are outstanding spots for indulging in beautiful treats without sacrificing any sweet cake flavour.

BAKE-A-BOO

86 Mill Lane, NW6 1NL
www.bake-a-boo.com
020 7435 1666

Zoe Berkeley does not believe in over-complicating baking—just because a cake is vegan, gluten-free or even sugar-free, does not mean the recipe needs to be burdened with artificial ingredients. Simple substitutes and a desire to serve truly tasty treats have worked in Zoe's favour, and her tearoom based in a quiet corner of north London is a booming success. Of course, the cafe is a regular destination for the sweet-toothed with food allergies and intolerances, but bake-a-boo is more than just a specialist cake shop. Gossiping friends, hen parties and locals seem unperturbed by the innocence of the cakes, and in love with bake-a-boo's nostalgic, prim and proper aesthetic. Net curtains, doilies and a dozen hanging chandeliers have been carefully arranged, while a private room at the back is set out like grandma's living room. While it may be a bit twee for some, it is certainly not contrived. Berkeley's personal touch is everywhere: 1930s film stills starring her granddad, Ballard Berkeley, hang on the walls; her sister's food photography is on display; and shelves of cards and crafts made by friends are available to buy.

Afternoon and cream teas book up months in advance, but pop in and you will usually find space to sit with a pot of old fashioned W Martyn loose leaf tea (or a bagged cup by Brewhaha) and one of bake-a-boo's luscious gluten and dairy-free Roxy raspberry cupcakes or a slice of sugar-free apple and date loaf—just two glorious fancies on an expansive menu.

cakes
bake-a-boo
BAKERY COOKBOOK
bake-a-boo
WHEAT, GLUTEN & DAIRY FREE
'Poppy'
blueberry & passion fruit
cupcakes

THE LANESBOROUGH

Hyde Park Corner, SW1X 7TA
www.lanesborough.com
020 7333 7254

Inspired by a friend who found it almost impossible to eat out and maintain her strict dairy and gluten-free diet, pastry chef Tal Hausen vowed to create a series of very special afternoon teas. Her sincere attempt to make them as beautiful and delectable as the traditional option is clear, and the chef has set the standard for London hotels wishing to follow suit.

Vegan, gluten-free and dairy-free diets are all catered for and Hausen has come up with an exceptional range of sandwiches and cakes working within tricky parameters. Depending on your specific dietary requirement, you can choose from specialist breads and flat wraps along with interesting spreads (a Parmesan-free pesto) and combinations (beetroot and avocado). Meanwhile vegans should brace for a triumphant chocolate cake—a sensationally rich, moist number. Gratifyingly, the tofu-based mousses are almost indistinguishable from their dairy-loaded counterparts, and the lemon and poppy seed loaf is unexpectedly light and bouncy for a flourless recipe. The scones, notoriously difficult to ace, are sadly a little lacklustre. But this bespoke afternoon tea is still a resounding success. Part of the credit must go to the informed tea menu designed by acclaimed tea 'sommelier' Karl Kessab, as well as the divine and refined Apsleys restaurant where a magnificent glass roof bathes the room with light. Lounge chairs, attentive service and a live pianist complete the picture, making any afternoon tea here a real indulgence.

MS CUPCAKE

408 Coldharbour Lane, SW9 8LF
www.mscupcake.co.uk
020 7733 9438

Ms Cupcake's philosophy—that everyone deserves good cake—has made this fabulous bakery a huge hit. Mellissa Morgan (who channels a charismatic 1950s housewife) is behind the Ms Cupcake alter ego and beneath her glitzy, sugarcoated image, lies a home baker with a dream of making tasty treats for all. After turning vegan before launching this enterprise—and not one to let anything get in the way of a good cupcake—she set about devising sweet substitutes. She travelled to America and back home to Canada (where she says every city has a vegan bakery), and brushed up on her baking skills. She now has more than 100 cracking (sometimes crazy) cupcake recipes under her belt.

In her Brixton boutique, flavours on rotation include and The Ambassador (a cheeky salute to the Ferrero Rocher); there are also gluten, soy, sugar and wheat-free options available. Mellissa comes from the school of baking that promotes equal parts sponge and frosting as the ideal ratio, so these are not for vegans looking for wholesome cakes. Excess is the theme here, and despite the pure sounding ingredients (almond milk, rice flour, fruit purees), the cookies, doughnuts and pies are all about indulgence.

Ms Cupcake

THE GALLERY CAFE
Breakfast Menu: until 11:30am
Day Menu: 11:30am - 3:30pm
Day Menu: 11:30am - 3:30pm
Evening Menu: 3:30pm - Close
ALL FOOD IS VEGETARIAN OR VEGAN

THE GALLERY CAFE

27 Old Ford Road, E2 9PL
www.stmargaretshouse.org.uk
020 8980 2092

The Gallery Cafe shares the same Georgian building as St Margaret's House Settlement—a charity that offers office space to more than 30 other charitable organisations—and it ploughs all its proceeds back into that good cause. The food matches the venue's earnest credentials by virtue of being entirely vegetarian and vegan, with plenty of juicy salads, quiches and stone baked pizzas on the menu as well as freshly baked artisan breads.

The cake selection is brief, and on busy days can sell out astonishingly fast. It is a shame, because the vegan chocolate cupcakes with mint icing are stellar, as is the moist banana loaf and walnut-heavy brownies. You will always be sure of a cup of tea, however, with loose specialities from Covent Garden's Tea House ranging from Lotus Blossom to Lapsang Souchong. The garden-backed conservatory or front terrace are ideal spots for sipping tea and eating cake during the day, while from dusk, the indoor sharing tables come alive as The Gallery Cafe turns into something of a community arts venue with weekly open mic nights, gigs, film screenings and even a world music festival in March.

42º RAW

6 Burlington Gardens, W1S 3ES
www.42raw.com
020 7300 8059

From its base at the Royal Academy's sister space, 6 Burlington Gardens, 42º Raw hopes to bring its raw food philosophy to the mainstream. Its Danish founders—who originally launched the concept in Copenhagen—believe in 100% plant-based food, where no ingredient is heated above 42 degrees Celsius. The uncooked fare is also limited by 'no sugar' and 'no dairy' stipulations.

The savoury menu reads simply enough: there is a colourful salad bar, inventive sandwiches and creative veg dishes. But when it comes to cakes, the cafe has had to overcome some major challenges. Tarts appear to be the way around the non-baking issue: chocolate, strawberry and chocolate-mint tarts are on offer daily, made with a pumpkin or sunflower seed base mixed with coconut butter or oil. The mousse-like filling is made with natural oils, nuts, cocoa powder and fruits, making the finished product (packed with antioxidants and healthy fats) genuinely good for you. There is no getting around the fact that they taste different to butter and sugar-loaded sponges, but there is still a satisfying sweetness to the tarts that make them a worthy treat for dedicated raw foodies.

POGO CAFÉ

76 Clarence Road, E5 8HB
www.pogocafe.co.uk
020 8533 1214

Although Pogo Café is not solely dedicated to serving tea and cake, it is committed to catering for special diets as well as those with a social conscience. It is vegan through and through and, run as a co-operative, it is entirely reliant on voluntary workers. Veganism is heavily promoted here, and the shabby cafe is a hub for meetings, benefits and debates about the lifestyle choice as well as socio-political film screenings and talks about topics such as "practical squatting". It may sound worthy, but Pogo is not as po-faced as you might think.

The menu is a colourful mix of tofu burgers, nachos and banana splits, while the cakes have become legendary. With different volunteers working in the kitchen each week, the selection is always a surprise. But keep your eyes peeled for the regular rich cherry and chocolate cake or the dense mango cake (which is as good as a butter and egg-free sponge will allow). The slightly chaotic food counter also features an array of bagged and branded teas as well as a choice of sweet soya milkshakes.

VEGANCAFE

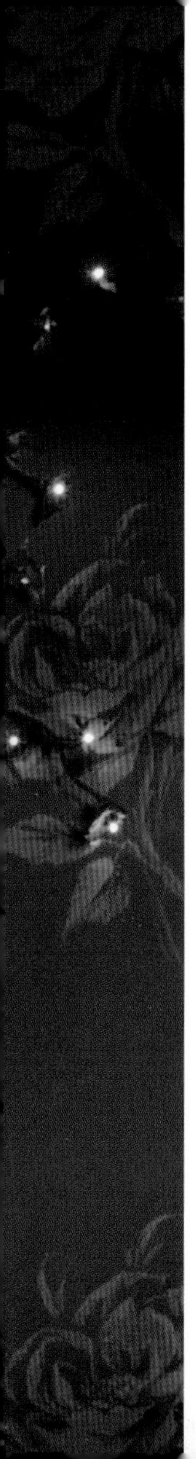

THANKS

People often ask me, "Where is the best place for tea and cake in London?" It's a tough question to answer, and I usually end up dodging it with the truth: it really depends on what sort of experience you want. There are so many ways to take tea in the city, from an unceremonious shopping break to a dress-up-and-dine celebration. But I hope that this guide provides a tea and cake solution to suit every occasion and mood. I've certainly endeavoured to make the final cut as diverse as possible, and looked to mingle a few surprise spots among the more iconic destinations. I truly hope you've found the selection inspiring, and that it has helped you discover a few new prized places to enjoy the simple pleasures of tea and cake.

In compiling *Tea & Cake London* I have met some wonderful cafe owners, bakers, waiting staff and PRs and I'd like to thank them all for their enthusiasm and willingness to have their venues featured on these pages. I'd also like to thank my publisher Black Dog for having faith in my idea, as well as my parents, siblings and friends for their help in sampling cake! I'm particularly indebted to my most beloved champions, Steve and Mum.

Black Dog Publishing Limited
10A Acton Street
London
WC1X 9NG

t. +44 (0)207 713 5097
f. +44 (0)207 713 8682
e. info@blackdogonline.com.
www.blackdogonline.com

Designed at Black Dog Publishing by Leonardo Collina

ISBN 978 1 907317 48 4

Photography credits: Leonardo Collina at Black Dog Publishing pp. 6–13, 18–55, 58–65, 68–71, 74–103, 112–117, 128–137, 140–151, 158–162, 166–171, 174–179, 182–189. Georgia Glynn Smith pp. 16–17. Mariann Fercsik pp. 56–57. Keiko Oikawa pp. 66–67. The Original Maids of Honour pp.86–87, The Lagham pp. 106–107. Sketch pp. 122–123. Steve Pill pp. 120–121, 156–157, 186–187. Benjamin CM Backhouse pp. 137–138. Tom Watkins p.163 (above). Daniel Gianini p.163 (below).Kim Lightbody pp. 172–173.

Cover design: photography and design by Leonardo Collina.
Venue and props courtesy of High Tea of Highgate.

Black Dog Publishing is an environmentally responsible company.
Tea and Cake London is printed on FSC accredited paper.